A Love Journey

He Said

She Said

A Love Journey

Written by:
Gloria Angelou & Derric McIntosh

We decided to write this book because it tells an interesting story about how love is unfailing. We have heard that love is not supposed to hurt, however, this story doesn't lack pain or heart ache. One thing we came to find in our journey to love is that it wasn't easy, but it was certainly worth it.

Frederick Douglass once said: "If there is no struggle, there is no progress." The struggles that we endure are not for nothing, there is power in pain.

Gloria & Derric

To those who have given up on love, I say 'Trust life a little bit.'

Maya Angelou

She Said

Chapter 1:
First Sight

1998 freshman year. My first day of high school was focused on not getting beat up for being light skinned, having freckles and talking white—let alone being named after my grandmother, Gloria Nichols. The jokes seemed to create themselves. I've always been a little different and people seemed to hate that about me. I had never fit into a typical clique. Not smart enough for the nerds. Not mean enough for the bullies. Not black enough for the black folks. Not even white enough for the white folks. Even still, I did everything I could to try to fit in, but peers were quick to see my shortfalls and call them out as if they were one of the deadliest sins. I had the hardest time friending black girls. They automatically thought I wanted to compete with them in some way, and I had no clue I was even in the running. Hell, I didn't even get titties until ninth grade, so I never considered myself to be a threat.

To make the transition to high school easier, I had tried out for cheer squad the summer before school began. I'd figured most cheerleaders were popular and it might be easier to make friends if I made the team. *Everybody* liked cheerleaders, right?

I felt the cattiness right away at tryouts: the eye rolls because my bucks were above my shoulders, the snappiness from sophomores who thought they were irreplaceable, and the teeth sucking because I could bust all three of my splits without hesitation. The cheerleaders didn't like me, but nonetheless I made the team.

On my first day of high school, I was surprised to find that I was already well known. Upperclassmen knew me by name, some teachers were familiar with me, and even the cool police officer on school duty knew who I was. It wasn't long before I won a spot on homecoming court as the freshman representative. Even with the shadiness of my own teammates and the sassiness of some of my classmates, I still felt hopeful that my first year in high school would be great.

It was important for me to have notoriety. I never knew my father growing up, and my mother wasn't around much. I never felt like I received the attention that a child deserves. It was hard for me to identify with anything because I didn't know where I came from. I didn't have many men in my life, so naturally they became mysterious and interesting.

My relationships with boys always came easy. Boys were fun to be around, more free spirited than girls, and provided something I'd longed for my whole life—security. Before high school all my best friends were boys. Since they had never approached me in an intimate way, I knew the friendship was genuine. It could have had something to do with the fact that I looked like one of them.

Things took a drastic turn for me in ninth grade. I began to fill in noticeably. I decided to own my femininity a bit more. I noticed a difference in a few of my male friendships, some of which made me uncomfortable. I liked this type of attention, but I certainly wasn't trained for it.

My favorite part of high school was lunch. I would be lying if I said I didn't enjoy the food, but I would have definitely been shunned for admitting it at the time. However, the food was not why lunch was my favorite part of the day. Lunch equated to *freedom*. Kids would be in the halls surrounding the cafeteria and gym, just hanging out, talking, playing basketball, doing hair—all kinds of things. Most of the time I would watch the guys play basketball while being "fake" busy doing homework.

One of those lunch hours would change how I looked at love for the rest of my life. It was one of those fake busy days, and I'd put it on thick this time. I had the whole set up— humanities book, math papers, and even prescription glasses that I got from the bottom of my grandma's purse. I looked so studious, people had begun offering me money to do their homework.

One girl in particular, Mya, came over needing my seemingly genius assistance. She was a senior, but she looked like a freshman. She wasn't very developed physically and wasn't overtly sexual. Mya was friends with everyone. She was a bit of a tomboy, so she wasn't a direct threat to the popular girls, not to mention she was in the band and everybody liked band members. We'd talked sports a few times, since the band coordinated events with the football players and cheerleaders. She gauged my mood then proceeded to ask me if I had good handwriting.

Naturally I lied. I didn't want to disappoint. I wasn't sure why she was asking me about my handwriting, but I was willing to take a chance on helping her. She was nice and older and frankly, I needed a friend.

Mya led me to a group of seniors that were sitting in the hall by the lunchroom. I hadn't remembered seeing any of them in passing before, but I was flattered that I could possibly help an upperclassman. This group of guys seemed to be in a completely different category than I was familiar with. I couldn't really put my finger on it. They weren't jocks, but they didn't hang with the geeks. They seemed to create a new category of cliques, which in itself was cool. They welcomed me right away and seemed glad that I came to help solve this handwriting issue. Mya introduced me to a boy sitting on the floor named Derric. He was the one with the dilemma.

At first sight, I could tell Derric was a cute guy. He had a friendly, nice smile and wore an oversized blue polo shirt. He was quiet as Mya explained that Derric needed me

15

to write a note excusing his absence from school the previous day and to sign it as if I were his mother. He had decided to take a Ferris Bueller day and didn't want his mom to find out.

I began to feel nervous only because I lied about my handwriting. I had the handwriting of a seven-year-old, and that's on a good day. As I penned the fraudulent note, Derric gave me pointers on some of his mom's signature moves. (No pun intended.) I thought I did terribly, but I'd tried my best, and it seemed that Derric was happy with that.

As I handed him back the paper, he reached his hand up. The exchange seemed to happen in slow motion. He overextended his fingers a bit, which collided with mine. I instantly looked to see if it was just by happenstance. His right eyebrow arched as his lips formed a soft smirk. I looked away and bit my bottom lip with a slightly flirtatious grin. I wasn't sure what exactly was happening, but it felt good. Derric seemed different, ahead of his time even, which intrigued me.

I tried to walk away like I had some rhythm because I was pretty sure he and the rest of his friends were watching to see what I was working with. Feeling flustered, I quickly turned back around and told Mya something off the top of my head while walking backwards until I hit a corner. I couldn't handle that kind of pressure.

Apparently my strut hadn't been too much of a disaster. I saw Derric later that day and our eyes connected once again. Something about him was so different from any other guy I'd ever met. I just couldn't figure it out at the time.

He Said

Chapter 1:
First Sight

I spent the end of Summer 1998 partying and meeting girls. I was truly my father's son, but I had made a name for myself: Derric McIntosh bka D-Mac. My name was definitely ringing through the east side of town, if not other parts of the city too. I prided myself on my appearance, getting haircuts every six days, taking care of my skin, and dressing to impress. I wasn't into the normal urban gear my peers were wearing. I had a thing for Ralph Lauren and my sneaker game was always exclusive.

A good time seemed to follow me everywhere. I'd turned 17 that summer and met the rapper Xzibit in the mall, on my birthday. He invited a couple friends and me to hang out with him and Big Pun at the nightclub later that night, since I was celebrating becoming legal age. (Well, that's what my fake ID said anyway.)

That night was just another notch under my belt. I had been partying hard since I was 14, so essentially I was ahead of my time. The girls started to all look the same, wanting the same Capt'n, Save a Ho-type dude and giving it up to anything that looked like a bag of money. I wasn't that guy. I never let my left hand know what my right hand was doing, so I didn't attract many of those chicks, but the older ladies loved a little mystery. I lost my virginity to a older girl. I was 12. She was 17. I knew at that time I was on the fast track to bagging a MILF.

This was my last year of high school and I had done everything one could imagine. From drinking to girls, from partying to smoking... Those kids had no idea what fun really looked like. Their idea of a good night was going to an adult-supervised school function, only to get home by 9:45, talk on the phone and watch *Nick at Nite*.

I was beyond that. I needed to be stimulated in other ways, but since school was a requirement, I figured I would get this last year out of the way. My mom and I moved around a lot so I went to a few different high schools throughout my educational experience. She finally settled on Eastmoor when I was in the tenth grade. It didn't

19

make much of a difference to me. School was school. The good thing about the whole situation was that a couple dudes I knew from my previous high school, Abe and Trey, had also enrolled in Eastmoor. They became my road dogs.

Al was the brain of the group. That much was clear from looking at us. He was a tall, slim dude who wore glasses and graphic tees. The thing that stood out most about Al was his humped nose. That nose was so infamous, it had a whole separate name. We called it Biggie, after the late great, of course. The name seemed fitting. I think he even had to get a special shaped fitter so his glasses would sit on Biggie appropriately. Al looked goofy, but he still pulled girls. His personality saved his penis from drying up.

Trey was known as the dirty guy, and wasn't ashamed of it. He rarely showered, almost never brushed his teeth, and he would wear the same clothes often. Not to mention, he had a full beard in twelfth grade, but went long stretches of time without getting a haircut or grooming his hair. He always had a slight piss odor that probably came from the residual piss dudes have in their underwear from not shaking properly. It wasn't because Trey was poor or had a rough upbringing. He was just like that. The rest of his family was pretty normal so I had always assumed he was unapologetically unwashed. However, he was a monster in the studio. He could make a hot beat out of anything and drop 16 bars off the dome at any given moment. He often blamed his grime on grind.

Abe was definitely the alpha between him and Trey. I used to refer to Abe as Trey's dad because he did everything for him. Abe would take Trey to school and to get haircuts (and sometimes paid for them). He even got Trey jobs, like any good dad looking out for his son. The three of us were an interesting combination, but music is what connected us. We each had something powerful to bring to the table and it would prove to be a dynamic over the years.

School orientations were held just before school started. There were usually a lot of freshmen because they were new to the whole environment and needed help getting acclimated. Trey liked going to see the new "potential" or as Abe said, "fresh meat." I wasn't too impressed with the juvenile stuff. After all, I was a grown man now—or at least that's how I felt. But for entertainment purposes, I went.

We walked around the school like we owned the place. Trey contemplated pulling the fire alarm in the middle of freshman and sophomore talk time, just to get a better look at the prospects, but there was security manning every corner. We hung out for almost an hour before I got bored. Nothing was really happening and it seemed like the same shit, just a different year.

On our way out, I caught a glimpse of the cheerleaders. I was familiar with most of them except one in particular. I had never seen her before so I didn't know if she was just new or if she was an incoming freshman. I wasn't normally impressed by our cheerleaders because they all seemed out of touch and way too excited. That perky shit got on my nerves. Nonetheless, I was kind of taken aback by this girl. She seemed sure of herself and stood quietly at attention. I couldn't help but smile at the strategically placed freckles on her nose. I didn't feel like it was the best time to approach her, but I knew I would be checking for her when school started.

The first day of senior year wasn't too bad. I didn't have many classes so I wasn't there all day, which was good—I could go to school half the day and work the other half. Abe and Trey had a few more classes than I did, so they were there most of the day. At times I would hang out with them just for shits and laughs. I didn't normally patronize extracurricular activities, but I was looking for a particular cheerleader. It gave me an excuse to go to a couple games.

I only showed up to the rival games: Independence vs Eastmoor or Walnut Ridge vs Eastmoor. I knew a lot of people from Independence, more than I knew from Eastmoor, so I would always sit on the rival side. I saw the freckled cheerleader a few times and I grew increasingly curious every time I saw her. I did begin to feel a little like a creep, so I kept things chill.

My school schedule seemed to be working well until administration threw a wrench in my whole system. They decided to move homeroom from third period class to first period. I had study hall the first two periods of the day so needless to say, I didn't normally show up until later. Halfway through the year, I still wasn't adjusted to the new schedule. One night, I decided to party on campus—college girls go hard. I paid for it the next morning, and decided to cancel the whole next day.

This particular year, school staff didn't seem to let anything slide. As soon as I came back from my hiatus, my homeroom teacher was on my ass about having a note from my mom excusing my absence from the day before. Without that note, I would have to serve detention. I had forged my mom's signature many times, so when I showed up with a personally written note signed by Yours Truly, Ms. Thomas wasn't having it. She knew my writing and told me to try again. She advised me to at least have a different signature than my own. Clearly I didn't want my mom knowing I skipped school, so I decided to reach out to my fellow comrades. Abe pointed out that we had the same homeroom teacher and she knew his handwriting, so I thought I would just ask someone else.

I needed to have something suitable to give to Ms. Thomas by the end of the day. As it got closer to the last bell, I saw my friend, Mya, in the hall at lunch. Mya was a cute tomboy. She wore big clothes presumably to hide a body under there. She was sitting in the hallway when I approached her about my situation. She kind of laughed it off and said she couldn't help, but that she knew someone who might be able to. I wondered who she had in mind.

I went back and sat in the hall with my boys to do our usual clowning. It didn't take Mya long to come back. To my surprise, she came back with the cheerleader I had been eyeing since school started. I didn't even have time to stand before Mya's swift introduction: "Gloria, Derric. Derric, Gloria." And just like that we were formally acquainted.

Gloria. I should've known she would have a mature name. She seemed to be nervous, and honestly, her handwriting wasn't great, but it wasn't about how good or bad her handwriting was. It was about the handwriting being different from mine.

When we parted ways after that initial meeting, I thought about Gloria a lot. In just those few minutes, I found that I enjoyed talking to her. I picked up on her energy and thought we had a good vibe. The only problem was that she was a freshman.

Been there, done that.

She Said

Chapter 2:
Jack Pot

I made it halfway through my freshman year with only one fight. This, by the way, boosted my popularity. An Ethiopian girl, who called herself Cookie, wanted to try me one day in science class. I didn't know what her problem was, but I knew eventually we were going to have to box it out. It seemed as if my whole existence bothered her. No matter how nice I was, she always found a way to create a problem, and I didn't have time for that.

On this particular day, I had time. I wasn't in the best of moods. The previous night I got into a big disagreement with my mom and it had me thinking about other living arrangements, so I was at a point where I felt like I had nothing to lose. Science class was my first period, so it set the mood for the rest of the day.

As I walked in, the room was already full of students. I slid in right as the bell sounded. Mr. Stine, a stubby, older white man with long hair and bifocals, greeted me with a sly smile and an uncomfortable hug. Overlooking the fact that I was a straggler, he began to call attendance. As he approached my name, I could hear the heckling of Cookie and her peons behind me. When he said, "Gloria," Cookie proceeded to yell out, "that ho." As I stated before, I had time that day so I left no rock unturned. The first thing that came out my mouth was, "Ya momma's a ho." I took it a step further to cover all bases and get the crowd really going. "Ya grandma's a ho too." Anyone who grew up in the 90's knows "ya momma" was fighting words automatically.

Cookie stood up aggressively, but I was ready. In ninja form, I kicked the seat out in front of me to slow her approach. She stumbled over the quiet girl who sat behind me. This was my opportunity to gain control over the situation and do the most logical thing I could think of— grab her hair and drag her. While this was happening, all I heard around me was, "Get her ass," "Get up, Cookie," "Fight back, girl. You losing," "Aww hell naw, Cookie, she in that ass." I decided to let her go and give her a fair chance to whoop my ass like she said she was going to do. It never happened.

She got up, disheveled, and tried to run towards me like she was in a zombie apocalypse, but I had to Hadouken her back to the ground. Like I said, I had time. While she was there, I decided to get some boxing practice in and took all my past problems out on her face. Someone eventually broke us up and dragged me to the hallway. With all the commotion, I was overwhelmingly calm. I felt like whatever anger or aggression I previously had all left my body at that time. This was my first high school fight, and from what the spectators say, I was the clear winner.

I felt like Rocky when he reached the top steps of the Philly art museum... until reality quickly set in. *I am a cheerleader. My position is on the line.* If I was suspended, I could potentially sit out for the rest of the year.

Surprisingly enough, the fight was never reported to the office. Mr. Stine decided to deal with it in his own way and it seemed like he expected payback in return for his kindness. I played along, but the first chance I got, I was transferred out of his class and avoided him altogether.

Although Cookie and I were never reported, the news spread quickly. It eventually reached my cheer coach and she made me do extra laps, but that was pennies compared to the price I could have paid. I gladly ran two extra miles with a smile.

I saw Derric in the hall the next day after the fight and I tried to avoid him. Even though I was proud of my champ title, I didn't want to come off as a hood rat to a guy that I just met. He didn't give me a chance to run. He called my name like he was a drill sergeant in the military. I stopped abruptly and slowly turned around.

"Oh hey, Derric. I didn't even see you." Lying my ass off.

He ignored the mendacious remark and proceeded to address me as "killa." I laughed it off and quoted the late great Tupac and said, "Ha ha, I'm not a killa, but don't push me." Clearly, he heard about my victory and wanted to celebrate with me.

As he spoke, I noticed he had a quiet confidence about himself and a seemingly laid back style, which I wasn't sure how I felt about quite yet. I was used to loud boys and athletes, people who stood out in a crowd. Nevertheless, I was intrigued. We exchanged pager numbers and he told me he wanted to take me out one day. I was still trying to decide if he was genuine or if he was just looking for some fresh meat. He seemed like one of those guys that hung around new class orientation just to get the pick of the litter. Even still, I agreed to go out with him. He was a senior. How could I turn him down?

After my fighting victory, I needed a break from my inner city peers. I bounced around a lot, but there had been a previous period of my life when I was steady for at least two years and was able to establish some everlasting friendships. My best friends were boys because I believed I needed their comfort and covering at that time. I had gone to a different school district most of middle school. That school district was mostly white people, but they were a unique kind of white people. Blackish. I think that's where I felt the most comfortable and the most welcomed.

While in middle school, I met Mike, Julius, Justin, Tommy, Lejuan, and D'ario. That was the crew. When I hung with them, it felt like love. They were the brothers I never had. We would often hang over at Mike or Julius's house.

Julius was the clown of the crew. He was tall, black as hell, and skinny. I admired him and Mike because as young kids they would preach the gospel, carry around Bibles, and give you the business if you got out of line. I knew nothing about the Bible. I wanted to know, but I was never taught. Being around Mike and Julius gave me an introduction to the Lord in ways I didn't realize until I grew up.

As much as they loved the Lord, we were still kids and lived carefree most of the time. Mike was my favorite out of the whole crew. He was the most mature, the most athletic, (the cutest), and the wisest out of the guys. I loved Mike like a brother and I held a special place for him in my heart.

The Saturday after the infamous fight, I got to hang with the old crew at the mall. We went downtown to City Center and let loose. I seemed to forget all about my teenage problems when they were around and I became a free person.

Not long into our mall adventure I saw Derric. We locked eyes once again and he waved me over. I told the crew I was going to talk to this guy I knew from my high school, but they weren't having it. In big brother fashion, they all marched behind me as if we were facing off in a dance competition. Derric wasn't shook at all. In fact, I think he thought it was cute, in a protective kind of way. I introduced the boys to Derric and they all dapped him up, taking a couple minutes to read him, then gave their blessing. I left with Derric. Unofficially, this was our first date.

Derric and I hung out for a while and browsed the stores. We talked and got to know each other better. We sat down in the food court area and talked for a while before I noticed a group of guys looking hard in my direction. They were trying to get my attention and clearly had no regard for Derric. Conveniently, Derric got up to go to the restroom. I gave one of them a cute, little shy smile and indirectly invited him over. I liked the attention and this was a good time to see if Derric had any spunk in him. Although I was nervous for his reaction, I needed to see if he would be a good protector. I wasn't sure what that was supposed to look like in this situation, but I knew if I could look at his eyes, they would tell me everything I needed to know.

When Derric got back to the table, the group of guys were still there. One of them decided to pitch the obvious. "Oh my nigga, dis you?"

Without hesitation, looking the guy dead in his eyes, Derric confidently responded, "Absolutely."

His assertiveness was so sexy, I could have let him have it right there in the food court. I quickly stood up and grabbed his hand. I knew the guys would get more disrespectful so I led Derric away gently. After all, I had seen all I needed to see. I could tell Derric was little bothered by the confrontation so I held his hand into mine and brought him close to me.

I was trying to hide the fact that my heart kind of fell into my vagina and I started feeling warm things down there. I don't know why I got so weird. Maybe because it was the first time I had held a guy's hand in public or it could have been the fact that he was willing to fight for me.

As we browsed the mall, we came up on a gag store that Derric worked at. His friend, Abe, was working at the time. I almost thought he had one of those fake noses on that were attached to glasses, but to my surprise, that was his real nose. Abe seemed cool. He slid me some fake lottery tickets and Derric suggested I give them to my mom. Seemed like a good idea at the time. She was always playing the lottery, so I would just switch out one of her scratch off for a good laugh.

Before heading out, Derric grabbed my hand and pulled me under the escalator. He looked me dead in the eyes and told me he liked me. Without hesitation, I told him I liked him too. There was a brief moment of silence followed by what seemed to be a slow motion movie moment. He grabbed the left side of my neck and pulled me in to share a kiss that seemed to set off sparks. I opened my eyes in the middle of the intimate moment so I could see if he was all in it or if this was just game. His eyes seemed to be shut passionately as if *Gone With The Wind* were playing behind his eyelids. I knew at that point he really liked me, although I still had reservations about why.

Why did this seemingly established high school senior like me of all people? An awkward, insecure, damaged freshman. My trust level wasn't where it needed to be and I continued to look at him with a side eye expecting the rug to be pulled from underneath me at anytime. Instead of leaving me that night, he got Abe to drive me home. We sat in the back together and continued to kiss passionately. I couldn't help but open one eye to try to catch his friend being a creep, and there he was watching us in the rear view mirror. I quickly closed my eye and proceeded to give him a show. Derric and I became official that night.

He Said

Chapter 2:
Jack Pot

I spent a lot of time in the studio with Abe and Trey. We came up with some masterpieces that I felt were way underrated and overlooked. People weren't ready for the type of shit we were on. That's one thing about being ahead of your time—not everyone sees what you see, and by the time they do, you're on to some deeper shit. People appreciate that type of artistry now, but back then it wasn't socially accepted as well. I had aspirations of moving to California and being this huge music producer. I didn't see myself as having a wife and kids type dude. That seemed like a life that would conflict with my dreams. I didn't have time for a nagging chick at my throat going on about coming in from the studio late or having to stop what I'm doing to pick up little Jimmy from school because he's sick, or going to family functions that would require more than a few hours of my time.

I couldn't see anything more important than living that life, until that plan got thrown off by what I now know was God. I read an old Proverbs verse that said, "A man's heart plans his way, but the Lord directs his steps." I didn't understand this as a senior in high school, but I would soon learn I had less control over my life than I thought, especially when there was something that was meant to occur. Most of the time, I was standing in my own way.

I think I avoided the desire for family life because of how I saw my mother struggle to raise me independently. My mother and father had gotten a divorce when I was three. When he left, it seemed like he divorced me too. The best way I could describe my father was in the words of Tupac, "No love for my daddy 'cause the coward wasn't there." I never wanted that to be my story. History has a way of repeating itself and I wanted to avoid that generational curse. I was angry at my father. I spent a lot of time trying to figure out why he didn't love me enough to come around. What did I do in order for him to be so upset with me as a child as to not want me?

I never felt good enough, and although I never expressed that to anyone, it showed through my actions. I was afraid to take risks with the fear of rejection. I wouldn't try certain things because I didn't want to be thrown out of my comfort zone, and most of the time my sadness would be mistaken for softness, which would get some people fucked up. I was quiet, but I wasn't weak. The middle of my senior year would prove to be a life changing experience on how I went from an aspiring jet setter, music producer, kid-free bachelor, to connecting my mind with my heart to desire a different life altogether.

In the weeks after Gloria and I met, I noticed that whenever I would see her in the hallways, she would always make it a point to say hi to me. It wasn't just me noticing her anymore and I started to realize that maybe she liked me. For some reason, I got excited about that thought. I never was too invested on worrying about how a girl saw me because I never wanted anything long term. Things seemed different this time. I liked how she looked at me, as if I were the only guy in the room, like I was important, like I was worth coming back for. I came to school a period early just to get one extra smile from her and a "Hey Derric!" Those two things had me going for the rest of the day. Normally after first period, I would wait right at the corner of her science class as if I were coming from home room, but one day in particular she didn't pass by. Rumor had it that she beat the breaks off this chick named Cookie.

I knew Cookie. She was familiar with a lot of my dudes, which wasn't any surprise considering she was a cute Ethiopian chick with a body of a grown woman. She fit the description, but I was turned off by her loud mouth and ratchetness, so I never went there. (I thought about it a few times, though.) When I heard that Gloria tore Cookie a new asshole, I immediately smiled. Not because Cookie got beat up, but because I never expected Gloria to be a fighter. She was cool, pretty, and could hold her own? It was too good to be true. She was like a little black Chun-Li.

After I heard about the fight, I saw less of her. I asked Mya if she had talked to her and she said she had only seen her after school during practice, so I knew she hadn't been suspended. I decided that if I didn't see her soon, I would inadvertently bump into her after school.

Just as I was leaving for the day, I caught a glimpse of red hair and freckles. It was Gloria quickly walking by with her head down and eyes averted. I had to chase her down the hall and yell her name to get her to even look at me.. I wasn't sure why that would be. I thought everything was going well—after all, we had the best hallway relationship I had ever had before. When she finally turned around, I could tell something was off. She claimed she hadn't seen me, but I was the only other person in the hallway. I had never asked her if she had a boyfriend, so maybe she was in a relationship and all that *being nice* stuff was in my head. Or maybe she was just nice to everyone and I just felt like it was toward me. Could be she was having a bad day and didn't want to be bothered.

All those thoughts raced through my head as I tried to lighten the mood by calling her "killa." She seemed to loosen up a bit at that. When she recited the lyrics to Tupac's "Hail Mary," I could have married her right then. I decided to shoot my shot and ask for her pager number. I wanted to take her out that weekend, but I had to work.

I definitely had plans for her. I wanted to make her my girl right away.

I worked at the mall downtown, City Center, a huge mall that had two stories, underground parking and three large anchor stores. On Saturdays, it was poppin'. I liked working in the mall, not necessarily because of the people, but because I had a low-key shopping infatuation. Working at a place where all the newest sneakers dropped and the hottest clothes were displayed made it easy to access the things I wanted before anyone else.

One of those Saturdays right after I got off of work, I saw Gloria. She was on the second floor and I was on the first floor. I couldn't see who she was with, but it didn't matter much. I just needed to be in a position where she could see me and make it look coincidental. I ran up the escalator and sat down at one of the sitting areas pretending to read. Just as I hoped, she spotted me and yelled my name across the mall. It was like music to my ears.

I saw she was with a bunch of dudes, so I wasn't about to walk up on them. I waved her in my direction so I wouldn't be in the position to smack a nigga if I had to. She came over quickly as she led the pact. I stood up quick because I wasn't about to be caught slippin'.

Gloria introduced each one of the guys as her brothers, and although none of them looked alike, I was still relieved that none of them was her dude. After a few minutes of us talking, she told her brothers she was going to hang out with me. At first they didn't really jump on board with that idea, but eventually they loosened up and agreed to meet back with her later.

Gloria and I spent the rest of the day walking around the mall and talking. It sort of began to feel like a date, which I didn't mind. I was impressed with Gloria's conversation. She was a freshman in high school, but seemed more like a freshman in college. She could keep up with my rants about politics, and turn around and talk about who's who in hip hop. Where did this girl come from? She was like my very own Bonita Applebum.

As we were sitting at a table having a conversation about why Biggie was way better than Tupac, I noticed three guys walking by who seemed particularly interested in what was going on between us, or more specifically, with Gloria. As they walked by, I heard them say something under their breath, but I chose to ignore it. I could feel their eyes glaring at us and I knew there was going to end up being a problem. Being aware of my surroundings was a good thing, but sometimes I noticed shit that I wish I didn't.

I excused myself from the table to head towards the restrooms located behind Gloria's seat. I felt like this was another situation where niggas took my quietness for weakness and I needed to gather myself. I really wanted to see if she would feed into the bullshit or not. Loyalty was important to me. As I was walking back, I saw one of dudes sitting in my seat talking to Gloria. I didn't like that she was entertaining these niggas, but I knew how nice she was and I'm pretty sure they had manipulated her in some way.

When I walked up to the table, I stood there staring at the dude in my seat. He looked up at me and asked if he was sitting in my spot as if he didn't know I got up from there three minutes prior. I looked him dead in the eyes and I tried to give him the most surest, cockiest, absolute answer I could think of without blinking. He got up and moved along, but not before saying something slick. I really wanted to fuck him up, off the strength of his intentions. Seeing my agitation, Gloria grabbed my hand and told me that it was all right and that it wasn't worth it. At the end of the day, she was right, after all. She was there with me while he left with two dudes.

Unbeknownst to me, even if something popped off, I wasn't alone. My friend Rob was ducked off in the cut watching and waiting to make sure nothing went down. He walked straight up to me and let me know that he peeped the whole thing and had my back in case some dumb shit went down. Rob is that friend you definitely want on your side if it's about to get real.

After the drama was over, Gloria and I spent the rest of that day enjoying each other's company uninterrupted. We moved across the mall to somewhere more private. I wanted to be alone with her to tell her about these feelings I was experiencing. I knew that there was something special about her and I wanted to tell her she was one of the most beautiful people I had ever met, inside and out.

My 17-year-old self couldn't articulate or formulate the right combination of words to express how I felt in that moment, so I just told her I liked her and went in for a kiss. Her lips were so soft and I could smell the coconut oil and shea butter she used in her hair. It reminded me of all the important black women in my life and I knew right then I wanted her to be one. After we shared our first kiss, I asked her to be my girl, and she obliged.

We literally spent the whole day together and stayed until the mall closed. With her being my girl now, I felt that it was my responsibility to make sure she got home safe. Abe was working the second half of my shift and he was still there closing up for the night. I planned on hanging out with him after he got off, so the least he could do was give my girl a ride.

We walked back over to "Gags and Gifts," which was the novelty store where Abe and I worked. I asked if he would give Gloria a ride home and of course he agreed, especially when I offered five bucks on the tank.

I helped Abe clean and lock the store, and then the three of us headed to the parking garage. Gloria and I held hands along the way like a real couple. I couldn't believe that happened so fast. I hadn't wanted a real girlfriend since middle school, but for some reason, I couldn't let her slip away. When we reached the car, Abe got in the front seat, and Gloria and I got in the back. I kind of laughed to myself because Abe drove a '96 Cadillac Brougham, looking like Morgan Freeman in "Driving Ms. Daisy."

Gloria and I spent the ride to her house talking and kissing the whole time, never letting go of each other's hand. When we got to her house, we said our goodbyes and I knew immediately I was feeling a way that I had never felt before. I couldn't quite wrap my mind around it. She certainly had me at hello.

Chapter 3:
The Breakup

Derric and I were together for a few months before any issues occurred. We were pretty good together and I enjoyed being with him when we were alone. My biggest concern was his quietness. I took that for weakness and I was uncomfortable with that for many reasons, one of them being my need for security. I needed to feel protected in every situation. To me, that looked like constant aggression. The situation at the mall had me feeling like he had the potential to be a protector, but who the hell cares about potential at 14. I also felt invisible, which was a serious problem because at that time, I wanted to be noticed by any means necessary.

I needed attention in the worst way and felt incompetent without it. I got attention from Derric. However, when we would go out, he'd rather avoid people. I gravitated toward people and wanted to show off my guy, my outfit, or my new shoes. Not being very sociable bothered me. For that reason, people always thought I was flirting with them or their boyfriend. Truth be told, I just liked the engagement of conversation and the attention that it brought. I did get a lot of attention from the juniors and seniors, maybe because they were super sexually active and thought I might have been an easy target.

I hadn't officially given my virginity away and although I thought about it often, I was scared to death. Derric didn't even approach me one time in a sexual way. He didn't pressure me, or even discuss that type of intimacy, which honestly made me more curious.

Basketball season was the time where it seemed everyone was getting coupled up. The games were the big social event every week and everyone came out just to hook up. Since I was a cheerleader, I only got to hang out with the other cheerleaders during the game, and sometimes after the game the cheerleaders and basketball players would get together. There was one guy in particular, Chris Timberland, that I liked to talk to. He was pretty popular— point guard, dark skinned, white teeth, and dimples. He was the shortest guy on the team, but one of the best in the state.

He was safe. Always a gentleman. I would find myself engulfed in hour long conversations convincing him cheerleading was a real sport. Nobody took us seriously.

Although Chris was an interesting guy, there was another guy that caught my eye. He would be posted up by the school front doors with the same three guys and two girls, always wearing Girbaud jeans, slightly sagging, with different color Air Max sneakers every day. He had a distinctive laugh that made other people laugh and a smile that could light up any room. I never saw him at any sporting events. The only time I would see him was the first part of the day. After third period, he would disappear. I was so intrigued with him and I didn't even know his name.

I felt bad that I had these feelings because after all, I was with Derric, and he was a good boyfriend. Oddly enough, he made me want to experience consensual sex even more, and because he didn't pressure me, I questioned his sexuality. He also smoked weed. I couldn't really understand why or how such a seemingly good guy could resort to drugs. I felt like he was easily persuaded by others and I had zero tolerance for any kind of weakness. I really didn't want any part of his habit, but he promised he would stop. And I believed him, so it didn't come up again... until it did.

I found out the mystery guy's name was Kevin. I'd happened to see him walking in the alley behind my house and decided this was my chance to be aggressive. I walked up to the gate and as he got closer, I noticed he was freaking a Black 'n' Mild, so the first thing I said was, "You know smoking can kill you." He slowed down, laughed, and said, "Yeah, it's a bad habit." That's when I told him I saw him in school a lot and asked for his name. He put the Mild up to his lips and responded out of the side of his mouth, "Heaven." I was surprised. I told him I had never met a guy with the name Heaven. He chuckled and removed the Mild from his mouth and repeated himself: "KEVIN."

At that point, I was relieved. Heaven and Gloria didn't have much of a ring to it. I asked him where he was headed and before he could answer, I decided to reach. "Your girlfriend's?" He smiled with one side of his mouth and said, "Nah, nothing like that. Just my homegirl I smoke with." For some reason, I instantly became jealous. I almost forgot about Derric. Hypocritically speaking, Kevin made smoking look attractive.

At that moment, I made up in my mind that I needed to be Kevin's girl. He was easy on the eyes, he had facial hair, and his teeth were on point. He was mysterious in a bad boy kind of way and I liked that. He seemed to walk to the beat of his own drum, and I wanted someone who could lead me and teach me a few things, someone older and mature, but youthful and active.

I had to figure out how to break it off with Derric. I was having these feelings, but I didn't want to be the bad guy. I needed this breakup to be his fault so I could feel better about my selfish thoughts.

The next day when Derric approached me at school, I knew this was the moment of truth. He came up to me at lunch as I finished having my usual cheerleading debate with Chris. For some reason, Derric seemed upset and more aggressive than usual. His eyes were bloodshot and he reeked of weed. Oddly enough, his rebelliousness didn't have the same effect as Kevin's, so I took offense to his whole ambiance.

I waited for him to speak, and the first words out of his mouth were: "Are you fucking with Chris?" I paused and took in the aroma his breath gave off from the weed.

Instead of responding to his accusation, I decided to deal with the most pressing issue. "Nigga, are you high!?"

His eyes immediately dropped to the ground and his posture slumped over. Before he got a chance to respond, I attacked his character, reminding him of his promise to quit. Since he didn't uphold his end of the promise, I was done. I said all of that in one breath and walked away like Bernadine in "Waiting to Exhale" after she set John's clothes on fire and blew up his car.

In my head Derric ruined our relationship and because of that, I had reason to move on by any means necessary. My new mission: Operation Kevin.

He Said

Chapter 3:
The Breakup

It was exactly seven weeks and five days since Gloria and I had made it official. Then all hell broke loose. I felt her slipping away weeks before it actually happened, but I thought I was just trippin'. I didn't really know how to act around her. She made me feel soft, and I wasn't all the way comfortable with that. Dudes weren't supposed to be soft. We're supposed to be men. Be hard, be tough. She ignited feelings I didn't even know I was capable of having. I wanted to hide all the wild things about me that I thought might run her away.

I wanted to hide the fact that I was still smoking weed, but it had become a part of me. It took me to a place where I couldn't otherwise get to on my own. I wanted to hide my playboy ways because if she knew how I used to jump from one girl to the next with no regard, she might be turned off and think I would treat her that way. I never wanted to see her hurt, let alone be the source of her pain.

She was different than other girls. She talked different, she smiled different, and most of all, she looked at me different. When she looked at me, it was like she was staring straight through my soul and literally smiling at my heart. I had never been in love with a girl before, but I was sure that's what I was experiencing.

Gloria and I would often hang out at my mom's house. My room was in the basement. It was nice and private, almost like my own apartment. Her favorite pastime was watching romantic comedies and eating flavored popcorn, so I always made sure I had some Cracker Jack on deck. The thing I loved most about Gloria was the fact that she was so versatile. We could talk about hip hop moguls in one instant, then turn around and she was schooling me on pharmaceutical science.

One of her favorite movies at the time was *It Takes Two*. I'm not sure what the movie was about, but I know it had the twins from *Full House* in it, and every time we'd watch it, Gloria would cry at the end. It was a sappy movie, but one part I do remember, since I had to watch it at least five times, was when one of twins began describing love. She said, "It's gotta be that can't eat, can't sleep, reach-for-the-stars, over-the fence, world series kind of stuff." The first time I heard that , I thought it was the perfect way to describe how I felt about Gloria. I would quickly glance over at her while watching that part and each time she had a soft smile on her face and a gaze in her eye, indicating to me that she loved the idea of love.

The last time we watched that movie, I wanted to tell her that's how I felt, but my fears of rejection held me back. Instead, I just kissed her on her forehead and held her close to me. By now I would have smashed a random female and passed her to a homie, but I wanted to take it slow with Gloria. When I thought about sex with her, it seemed wrong, at least the way I knew how to do it. I wanted it to be right. I wanted it to be special. I didn't ever want her to feel like that's all I wanted from her.

I was surprised at myself. I was acting way out of character, but in a good way. She instantly turned me into the man my father never was, and I didn't want to go back to living in the mind frame that I had before I met her.

Prom was coming up, and even though it was my senior prom, I had plans on making that evening all about her. I was going to surprise her that week on our two month anniversary with some flowers and Baby Face playing in the background.

That particular weekend went well. I spent time with my girl, did some overtime at work, and kicked it with my boys. Monday would prove to change everything.

Trey and I decided to skip a couple classes to go to the mall and pick up the new Air Jordan XIV. Abe and I smoked on the way there. Trey didn't smoke so I made him sit in the back even though he had called shotgun. On our way back to school, I made sure to spray some Brut on so Gloria wouldn't catch a whiff of the weed. I was feeling good that day and couldn't wait to see my girl.

On the way back home, I told the guys I was going to make this the day I told her I loved her. Trey had some sort of issue with his throat every time I even mentioned Gloria's name. He would clear his sinuses as if he had a pubic hair stuck in his throat. I saw Trey and Abe make eye contact through the rearview mirror.

Abe shook his head and told Trey, "Don't do it."

However, Trey couldn't hold water and started telling me how he heard that Gloria and some nigga named Chris were rumored to be messing around. Trey insisted that I check her and make sure that I wasn't being played. I couldn't see Gloria messing around on me, but for some reason, I let him charge me up. After all, I was D-Mac. I don't get played... I do the playing.

When we got back to school, it was lunchtime and the three of us split up. Before Trey left, he patted me on the back and told me to handle my business. That pissed me off even more because he smeared chicken wing sauce on my Polo coat from the fried wings he had eaten. I hadn't seen Gloria yet that day and for some reason, I didn't see her in the hallway where we normally would meet. I decided to just chill and not let Trey's words get me worked up any more than they already did. I had bigger problems, like figuring out how to get that Asian Zing sauce off my coat.

Suddenly, Trey came running back to tell me that Gloria was in the lunchroom with Chris, flirting and getting a little too familiar with him. This got me hot again. Even though I hadn't seen it, the thought of my girl hugged up with another nigga made me see red. Who the fuck did this Chris dude think he was? He didn't want those problems. I was pumped up and talked myself into running up on the both of them.

As I got closer to the lunchroom door, Gloria was walking out. I let my emotions get the best of me and immediately asked her if she was fucking with Chris. Gloria had a surprised look on her face and I immediately regretted confronting her. She calmly said no, but quickly flipped it on me about how my eyes looked bloodshot. She asked if I was high. I wanted to say no, since technically my high had dissipated due to my blood pressure being up.

I just stood there, feeling like shit. I had promised her I wouldn't smoke again, because it seemed important to her. Even though I said I would stop smoking, all that really meant was I wouldn't let her "catch" me smoking. I looked at her and there was something different in her eyes—a look of disgust—and I knew it was over before she even said it. I closed my eyes to avoid seeing the words trickling from her mouth. "It's over." She seemed to say it in slow motion, and just like that, it *was* over.

I found myself pleading with her to give me another chance. I had never been in this position before. I had never cared enough about a chick to even tell them it was over, let alone stick around long enough to get broken up with. What was happening? Just to think a few hours earlier I was going to confess my love to her. Now I was standing there single, with a broken face, red eyes, and a greasy coat.

Chapter 4:
The Chase

I got in a lot of trouble being unattached. I was the type of girl who needed to stay in a relationship to avoid being called a ho. Every other week a new chick accused me of liking her man or she heard I did "this and that" with "such and such."

To be quite honest, I was pretty gullible, and gave into temptation quite easily. However, chasing after someone else's man had never been something I desired to do, not when these niggas were falling from the sky like water on a stormy day. They came a dime a dozen. So imagine my surprise when I found out Kevin had a girlfriend that lived away in college. I had a decision to make. Stick to my newfound morals and values, or forget everything I said about chasing someone else's man... I decided for the moment to stay classy. After all, prom season was rapidly approaching and I needed to be available for the several offers I got for that special night.

One of the prom proposals was from a guy named Shane. Bald-headed dude, about 6'3", heavy set, not particularly cute, but he had a great personality. I had shop class with him and his twin brother. They reminded me of the guys from my crew. From the time we got into class, to the time the bell rang, there was non-stop laughter. Shane used to always talk about his crazy ex and tell us horror stories about the certifiable stuff she would do.

When he asked me if I would accompany him to prom, I was super hesitant. I had no time to be peeking over my shoulder for a dude that I wasn't that into. The way he explained his ex had me picturing Carrie, and we all know how that ends. No ma'am, no sir, no thank you.

Somehow the news circulated that Shane had asked me to prom and all of the sudden, we were "fucking." I hadn't even agreed to go with him, but now people were putting us together as a couple? This proved to be a problem. Apparently, him and the "crazy ex" never broke up. The next thing I know, I'm being held up by pencil point by some chick named Shante. I wasn't sure what to do because I wasn't clear on what I did. All I knew is I had a pencil shoved under my chin by a girl who obviously lifted weights because her arms were strong as shit. I decided to take a less aggressive approach with this situation because this girl was obviously disturbed.

I put my hands up to let her know that I surrendered–and in a hostage negotiation type way–I asked what her demands were. Tears started to flow from her face and the veins in her forehead begin to throb. She spoke to me through her teeth as she began to verbalize why I was being assaulted. She said she was Shane's girlfriend and was warning me to stay away from him. Out the corner of my eye, I saw Shane's big ass peeking around the corner of the gym trying to hide behind the glass door. He made no effort to explain himself or help me out of that situation. By this time, there was a crowd and because my pride did not supersede my humility, I ran. I didn't stop until I got to the third floor bathrooms that were never used except to smoke in. I knew people would laugh at me for running, but at the end of the day, I was still a cheerleader.

I ended up not going to prom my freshman year. I had too many senior girls who wanted nothing less than to see me be pumped up with pencil lead. I thought about letting Derric take me, but I shut that thought down because I wasn't sure how safe I would be even with him. I would have hated to go to an event and not be able to dance or socialize, not to mention that the idea of Derric getting dressed up in a suit seemed almost laughable.

I survived my first year of high school, but I wasn't happy. I wanted one of those envious relationships, the kind that people say, "Dang, they still together?" I wanted to be coupled up with a guy that matched my new fly.

Derric graduated and I didn't go see him walk. My focus was on other things. This particular summer had to be spent on a strategic plan to lock Kevin down. He was going into his senior year and I had exactly three months to secure the bag before school started back.

That summer I consumed myself with cheerleading. We had a new coach, Mr. Tide Tomas, and he was quite the character. He was a young, black teacher right out of college and stood 5'2" on a tall day. He wore small glasses with the chain attached and dressed very nautical and clean cut. He didn't seem very athletic and didn't know much about cheerleading, but he was up for the job. He would prove to be someone who liked to use his power to control people and manipulate situations.

I lived across the street from the high school so I would normally walk home after practice. Kevin's house was adjacent from the school, so when I left the building doors, I could see what was going on in his yard. There was always some sort of party going on at his house, or a bunch of friends congregating in the front, so I got a good sense that he was a sociable person.

One day I got a glimpse of his girlfriend and I was disgusted. I didn't picture him with "that." I did everything I could to villainize her because, after all, she was dating my future boyfriend. She wasn't particularly attractive, and to me, she carried herself like a boy. I wondered what he saw in her. I didn't think about it too long; I couldn't waste any more brain cells on the whys. I had to focus on the future.

Mr. Tide Tomas began to get more familiar and more curious about me in particular. I immediately thought he was a creep, but I couldn't express that because I didn't want to compromise my position on the cheerleading team. Instead, I just went with his shenanigans. At times I was flattered with the type of attention he was giving me, but he took it to another level. During practices, he would seclude me from the rest of the team to work on "hands on things." He would have me work on my tumbling, and spot me in places that didn't need spotting. At this point in my life, I didn't see this as abuse, more of a nuisance. I wanted to focus on Kevin, and Mr. Tide Tomas was standing in the way of that. He wanted me to call him Ted, and be less formal, but all I wanted to do is cheer without my vagina being held hostage.

The first football game of my sophomore year occurred and I was still single. All of my tactics to get Kevin's attention failed and he was still with his ugly ass girlfriend. This was his senior year and I didn't have much more time to make an impression. The first couple of weeks of school, I would see him walking with a girl in my class named Dominique. She was a goody two shoes, who made better than straight A's and was part of all the clubs in school. I was confused by why they would be walking to school together, since they were an unlikely couple. I assumed it must have been his cousin or a family member because I was damned if I let someone else slide in on my future man.

I decided to ask Dominique about Kevin and her relationship with him. She told me they were not related, but their mothers were good friends and they spent a lot of time together outside of school because of that. In my head, I rebuked that in the name of Jesus and plotted their social demise. I would do little things to interrupt their potential focus on each other. I'd come outside and walk with them, standing right in the middle of those two crazy kids.

I used more of an aggressive approach, always asking him about his girlfriend that was AWAY IN COLLEGE. I even walked with Dominique down to his house a few times to wake him up for school. I wanted to let her know this was a team effort.

After more than a month of me playing interference, Dominique stopped showing up. We still had class together and she seemed to avoid me there too. She seemed upset about something, but I didn't care enough to inquire. That mission was complete and now that I knew Kevin was open to letting other girls in, I jumped on the opportunity to seize the moment. I started showing up to his house early before school to wake him up. His side door would always be open because his mom would go to work early and leave it open for Dominique. Little did she know, I was the new Dominique.

Trying to balance schoolwork, cheerleading, a social life, and stalking was hard. I only added to the stress by getting a job. I started working at Kroger as a cashier. I thought I was hot shit because normally kids my age start off as baggers, but I shot straight past the peasant work and got promoted to the register. I wanted to make my own money. My mom would threaten to take away my pager or not pay the bill, and I figured if I paid my own bills, there wasn't much she could say. The only problem with that job was transportation. Although I was old enough to work, I wasn't old enough to drive, so I struggled to get to work.

Derric still called me on the regular and I made it a habit to talk to him often. It made me feel better about treating him like shit. He was too nice, and kept in touch with me no matter how I treated him. Sometimes I had to use that to my advantage so I could get to work or have a listening ear when I needed to vent. Derric was out of high school now and working at the mall full time. I knew he wanted us to pick things back up, but my curiosity for Kevin wouldn't allow me to reach back. A part of me wanted Derric around because he seemed to show interest in me whether we were together or not. In his eyes, I could do no wrong. I didn't have many friends or family that cared that much, and I needed a friend like that.

He Said

Chapter 4:
The Chase

  The weeks following the break up between Gloria and me were almost unbearable. I found myself practically begging for another chance, which was completely out of character for me. She wouldn't budge. At times wouldn't even look at me. I couldn't understand how we went from loving on each other to complete strangers in a matter of two weeks.

  It took some time for us to get back on speaking terms, but when we did, I was pumped. I tried to stay consistent with calling her every day. I knew she got home from cheer practice at 5:07 p.m., then she would turn on her favorite Destiny's Child CD, do chores, and finish her homework. I called her at 7:45 p.m. every night. I wanted to let her know I was thinking about her.

  I would always ask her what she ate. She loved food, but sometimes she'd skip a meal because she thought she was getting fat or she wanted to look a certain way in her cheer uniform, but I thought she looked perfect. She seemed to like the fact that I showed interest in the small things, but little did she know I cared about all things concerning her. I just didn't know how to tell her that.

One thing I loved about Gloria was her way with words. She wrote poetry and short stories. Up until I met her, I had never heard a girl with such rhythmic flow. She let me read her poem book when we were together. Her mind was just as beautiful as her outward appearance. She actually wrote a poem for me after we broke up. I don't know if she was sending me mixed signals or if I was just hoping we'd be getting back together. I always left from around her feeling like there was nothing that I could have said that was gonna be good enough for her. She was holding back for some reason. I didn't know how it was going to happen, but I decided to make it my mission to stick around and win her back. But until she came around, I went back to my old ways.

Prom was approaching. I spent so much time hoping Gloria would reconsider, that I didn't put much focus on finding a date. School activities weren't really my thing, but this was *prom*, my last official function as a high school student. Even if I considered not going, my mom would quickly kick that thought aside. My mom was big on memories, always telling me, "You only have one life to live, so do it big." For that reason alone, she wouldn't let me miss that opportunity to still be a kid.

I needed a date. I didn't want to ask anyone new—the thought of getting to know someone else literally made me sick—so I decided to ask someone familiar. My ex-girlfriend, Jakita, and I had talked about prom since middle school, so I felt like she was a safe option. Cute enough to tote around and take pictures with, but nobody I was going to be seriously involved with after that night. Jakita was attractive with brown skin, long hair, and was 5'3". She was everything I needed her to be in that moment: a crutch.

Secretly I enjoyed a little competition. I saw prom as a game. I had to dress better than you, my date had to look better than yours, my hair cut had to be tighter, etc. That night I tried to focus on having a good time, and although I felt like I won the superlatives, I still had a feeling of emptiness. I took Jakita home before prom was over. Her job was complete. I went home, changed and picked up Tanisha, my after-prom date. Needless to say, she temporarily helped me fill some voids that night.

Graduation day came and all I wanted was to hurry up and get that school shit over with. Gloria called me that day to tell me she was proud of my accomplishments and that she was going to try to make it to the ceremony. I could tell by her voice that she wasn't coming. She was infamous for stringing me along, and I let her. I was used to broken promises, so I didn't expect much in that regard.

I had a lot to think about going into adulthood. After graduation, I had some grown up decisions to make. My dream was always to move to California and work in the music industry, live the single life and collect cars. My world was literally turned upside down my senior year, and all I thought about was what it would be like to have a family. I decided to stick around Columbus and continue to work at the mall for a while. I gave myself two years to figure things out. At the end of two years, if I wasn't where I wanted to be, or who I wanted to be with, I was going to enlist in the military.

Chapter 5:
Daddy Issues

I attributed a lot of my pain to the fact that I didn't have a father growing up. My mom always said my father was white and I had 10 brothers and sisters. My life goal as far back as I can remember was to find my father. I would stare at men in public to see if there was any resemblance. My mom said he was a white man, with red hair and freckles, which had me thinking I was related to random white men I'd see in passing. I would never be bold enough to approach anyone, but I would imagine a life with a two-parent home, in the suburbs, with a white picket fence and a big backyard. I imagined my siblings and me fighting over clothes and boys, and my brothers being overprotective as I went to school dances and first dates.

Along with developing a strong imagination, my daddy issues created a void I would try to fill with other males. That might explain my need for attention, and my interest in boys at an early age. Although I loved my father, before I ever met him, I was mad at him for not protecting me from the sexual abuse I had endured growing up. I believed I was a target because the predators knew I was vulnerable and fatherless. They didn't have anyone to fear or fight off. It was just me. Five-year-old me, seven-year-old me, ten-year-old me. I never told anyone about most of my sexual abuse because I was more afraid of my mom thinking I put myself in promiscuous situations. So I simply embraced the sexual abuse and pretended it was love. I wanted to be loved. I wanted someone to look at me and see all the wonderful things about me that the Bible said God saw in me, but I settled for lust and attraction.

While my first official consensual sexual experience was in high school, I had several encounters in middle school, even an accidental insertion. That completely freaked me out because as soon as his little, pink, undeveloped penis rubbed against my lady parts, I immediately felt pregnant. I was too young to be a mother, I thought. I hadn't even started my period. I put myself in compromising situations because I thought if a boy was sexually attracted to me, I must be special. No one told me otherwise.

I liked older boys; they made me feel safe. When I got to high school a lot of the upperclassman wanted to take my consensual virginity. No one knew I had been sexually abused or touched in any way, and in my mind, I was allowed to push the reset button.

After Derric and I broke up, I reached back to a few prom offers I'd received earlier on. My top pick was Dustin Johnson. He was a popular guy, football player, nice smile, but his face was an acquired taste. I told him I was available for that offer if he still wanted to take me to prom. He acted as if he was grateful and told me he wanted to go on a date before prom to "get to know each other better." I obliged.

We ended up going to Applebee's and he cut right to the chase. He wanted to be my "first." The idea seemed to excite him as he wrapped up the date and escorted me to the car. I started to get cold feet as he pulled into an empty parking lot across the street from another high school. I thought we would at least go to his house or somewhere more private. As he shuffled through his *112* CD, looking for the perfect song to take my "virginity," my heart started to pump so hard, I could feel it through my ears. All the windows were up and no air was circulating. I was already hot and I was concerned about my perm sweating out.

He finally settled on track 7, "Anywhere." This, I guess, was fitting seeing as were literally in the middle of nowhere about to have sex in a small 1994 Chevy Cavalier. I noticed he put the song on repeat, indicating the experience would be longer than 4 minutes and 4 seconds. We started kissing and for a brief moment, I opened my eyes, only to catch him staring at me. He didn't close his eyes when I opened mine. He just stared.

He leaned my seat all the way back and attempted to pull off my skorts. His arms weren't long enough to reach all the way across and down, so naturally I had to help. I thought there was no turning back; bottoms were off, windows were fogged, condom was on, which by the way I think he was wearing since we left Applebee's because I never saw him put it on in the car. The experience lasted through the first play of the track. We were headed back to my house by the time it was able to repeat.

I pushed reset on that experience too. In my mind, it never happened. I didn't feel anything magical, nor did I see hearts in my eyes. The only good thing that came out of it was the free meal. I was disappointed, but I was still fueled by the attention. I felt like he chose me for a reason and that made me feel good.

He Said

Chapter 5:
Daddy Issues

I was born to a teenage mother. Both my parents were 19 when I was born, but my father showed his age more than my mother. They met in high school, ironically at Eastmoor class of '79. I was born out of wedlock, but after joining the Air Force right after high school, my father decided to marry my mom. My father, Mark Herbert McIntosh, did surprisingly well in the Air Force. He scored so high on his ASVAB test that the recruiter went to his mother's home to personally tell her how well he did. My uncle brags about my father's achievements to this day.

When I was two, my father was stationed in California and received orders to go to Guam. That's when he came back to Ohio to marry my mother, and we accompanied him to Guam where we lived for two years.

During those two years, my father was quite the ladies' man. We were on a small island and part of an even smaller military community. Everyone knew everyone else's business and on several occasions, my mom was humiliated with stories of infidelities regarding my father. She got STDs more than once and finally got the courage to call it quits. She divorced my dad as soon as we got back to the States. Although I didn't have any recollection of the pain my mother went through, as I got older, I could empathize with the feeling of great loss.

I didn't see much of my dad after that. My mom and I were living with her parents on the east side of Columbus and I can remember life being pretty comfortable. There were times I felt an overwhelming sense of sadness because I missed my dad. I didn't understand why he wasn't around at that time, and I remember crying myself to sleep some nights calling out for him.

One thing about my mom, that I have grown to respect, is she never said anything bad about my father; she only tried to console me. I didn't know she was in just as much pain seeing me go through life without my dad. As I got older, I got more bitter and eventually numb. I realized my father chose to stay away. When my mom divorced my dad, he decided to divorce me, his baby, his only child. I went from bitter, to numb, to angry.

The few times that I did see him were for very short periods of time and he had no patience for me. He eventually became "Mark" to me. He didn't deserve a precious title like, "Dad." There were times he came into town and never told my mother or reached out to me in any way. We would find out after he left town through my uncle who he stayed with when he dropped in.

I found out he had a girlfriend in the same city we lived in and would frequently come to see her. I took that personal. Whenever he decided to come see me, he would come bearing gifts, usually sneakers. If he only knew I couldn't be bought. The price he would pay for his negligence would be greater than any gift he could ever give me. I never understood how he was okay with not wanting to be in my life at all. I found myself wallowing in my own tears as I watched an emotional episode of *The Fresh Prince of Bel-Air* when Will's dad came to visit and, in true form, abandoned Will again by running out on him. I felt every emotion, every tear, and every disappointment. I felt as if Will took a page from the story of my life and put it on screen for the world to see.

I found solace from the women in my life. My maternal grandma had four girls and always wanted a son, and out of all her grandchildren, I was her only grandson; so needless to say, she treated me a little differently than my girl cousins. I didn't mind that at all. I needed the extra love and attention. I tried to seek out my grandfather for the things my mother couldn't provide, but he kept his distance and never connected with me in a loving way. I felt the same kind of withdrawal from him that I felt from my father, and I started avoiding him as much as possible.

I felt abandoned by all of the male figures in my life, with the exception of Mark's brother, my uncle Derric. I was named after him and it's almost as if he should have been my dad. He taught me how to ride a bike and came to all my baseball games. I've always been able to talk to him about anything, even the growing hatred I had for his brother. He allowed me to vent and even bought me a heavy bag so I could box out my frustrations. I respected him and I valued his teachings.

It was hard being a boy in a family full of women with the pressures of becoming a man, without all the essential tools. I felt lost at times and internalized a lot. Uncle Derric always said real men don't cry, so in an effort to become a real man, I kept my emotions to myself. Because of my father's absences and my grandfather's insistence that I would never amount to anything, I found myself looking up to the wrong type of men.

Chapter 6:
Inter-Smitten

Sophomore and junior years were turning points in my life. I finally got my guy, and we were a thriving couple. It took a lot of hard work and manipulation, but at the end of the day, Kevin broke up with his college girlfriend and gave me his full attention. He broke up with her shortly after his prom, so I missed the mark to make an appearance with him on his last big social event. I wasn't worried about it because my senior year was approaching and I would make sure we were the next big thing.

I was having a lot of trouble at home and at school. I was constantly skipping school at the end of my sophomore year to hang out with Kevin and completely neglected some of my responsibilities. I barely made it out of 10th grade with a 1.8 GPA. Cheerleading was getting to be a burden because I spent too much time away from Kevin, not to mention Coach Tide Tomas was not letting up on being a creep. The summer going into junior year was the worst year of his creepyism. During cheer camp, Tide Tomas got upset with me because Kevin came to one of the cheer events and he figured he was the reason I was blowing him off, when in all actuality, he was a teacher, I was a student and I just wasn't interested. I liked older guys and maybe in a different circumstance I would entertain him, but I was not looking to become the next news headline for inappropriate teacher-student relations.

Coach started treating me different. He excluded me from some important cheers, and on several occasions, threatened to hold me back from competition. For a while I complied with most of his demands, rather it be meeting him for a one-on-one in his "office" or allowing him to "train" me further on my tumbling, so he could get a feel of my intimate parts and satisfy his need to be pedophilic.

One Saturday I was late to practice and all hell broke loose. Coach yelled at me in front of the other girls and told me I would suffer consequences for my tardiness. He then told me to go in the hall away from the other cheerleaders, so he could explain to me what my punishment would be. I didn't understand why he was so upset about me being a few minutes late; I was always late. When he got in the hall, he whispered in my ear and said, "I want you. TONIGHT." And licked the side of my neck. I took a step back, wiped off my neck aggressively and told him no.

As I looked to the ground, fearful of what might come next, I quickly reminded him I had a boyfriend and I just wanted to cheer. He let out a snide laugh through his nose, started clapping his hands slowly and said, "Well... con-grad-u-lations. I hope your little boyfriend is worth not going to competition." I looked up and saw the taunting smirk he usually had when he knew he had the power and I would cave in, but this time I didn't. I pushed past him to get my bag and ran straight home. I cried the entire way there knowing I just gave up the only piece of my social life I had at school.

I reached home and buried myself in my pillow. My face was swollen and my eyes were red when my mom came down the stairs to see why I returned back home so soon. I thought about lying and saying practice was cancelled. I didn't trust my mom with information; she always had a way of turning things back on me. However, my heart only let my mouth flow freely, and so immediately, I busted out crying again. I told her I wasn't allowed to go to competition because Coach was mad at me, and in a probing way, she asked why he would be upset with me. I told her he was mad that I had a boyfriend. You could tell by the look in her eye and the vein in the middle of her forehead that she was in fighting mode. I noticed her cheeks jumping from her teeth clenching and she finally asked, "Is this why he has been calling here late at night?" I lowered my head and nodded.

Immediately she grabbed her purse, the one with five different maces hanging from the side, and left out the side door. I slipped on some house shoes and ran eagerly behind her. I tried to ask her what she was about to do, but all she said was, "This muthafucka dun lost his mind, he got the right one today." As we approached the gym doors, I could see the girls on the floor stretching for mounts.

My mom swung the door open and didn't even get in good before she yelled, "YOU LITTLE PERVERT ASS NIGGA, YOU FUCKED WITH THE WRONG ONE!" Everyone was confused as my mom reached for all five of her maces. Coach nervously jogged out the opposite side of the gym and my mom ran after him. She came back several seconds later, out of breath. She grabbed me by my arm and said we'd go home and call the police.

My mom filed a report that day, but I didn't cooperate to the fullest. I just wanted it to disappear because I knew the wrath I had to deal with at school. When I got back Monday morning, none of the cheerleaders talked to me and some of the staff were standoffish too. The rumor was I made up some lies about Coach because I didn't make the competition team and I was mad. That was far from the truth, but since no one knew of his perverted and controlling ways toward me, it would seem as if I was trying to destroy him. There was a meeting for all of the parents of athletes, which informed them of the situation and let them know there was an investigation being held. Because of the investigation, we had to forfeit competition. The parents of the cheerleaders were livid. They did everything they could to get the staff to reconsider, but it never changed.

At home, things also got worse. My mom fell back into her old ways with drugs and alcohol and we fought every night. I felt like she hated the sight of me. Every time

I'd pass her, she would call me a ho or bitch. Granted, she did catch Kevin and me in the basement having an intimate night. At 15 years old, I had no business burning candles and running showers for my boyfriend. I didn't feel like that deserved a punishment since it was clearly a cry for attention.

The last straw was when my mom almost choked me out, her words ringing heavy in my ears: "Die, bitch." I knew I had to get out of there somehow, or else I *would* die. I bit her as hard as I could and her reaction enabled me to get from underneath her. I knew once she was off me, I could outrun her, and I would be safe. I busted out the side door and didn't look back.

It was raining that night and I was barefoot and shirtless. My mom ripped off my shirt as I got away and I was running down the street in my bra and cheer shorts. I ran to Kevin's house without hesitation. He had a scared look on his face when he came to the door. He asked me what happened, and I just melted in his arms and began to cry again.

As soon as I stepped in, headlights began to light up the house in front of me. It was his mom, so he instructed me to stand in the kitchen while he ran and got me a shirt. I felt anxious just standing there; I never had met his mom formally, and I didn't think this was the greatest moment to do so. As I stood soaking wet and shirtless in the kitchen, I saw a phone on the wall and thought it would be a good idea to pretend to call someone so I wasn't just standing there when she walked in and saw me shirtless. I picked up the phone, and dialed Derric's number.

I didn't expect him to answer, but when I heard his voice, I quickly hung up. Kevin's mom walked in, stood there, and yelled for Kevin. She asked why there was a "naked little girl" in her kitchen and proceeded to head upstairs. I dialed Derric's number again, and this time I just held the phone until Kevin came back with a shirt. He told me his mom said I had to leave, but at that moment, I had nowhere to go.

Kevin ended up dropping me off at a teen shelter, which was the best mistake he could have ever made. I was hurt because he didn't help me with any other options and I didn't feel protected. Nevertheless, this would be the beginning of my independence. The teen shelter contacted children services, which deemed I was in an abusive situation, and they quickly took custody of me. I had an option to go into foster care, but because of my age, the shelter had another option. It was a program called transitional living designed for 17-year-olds to help them get an apartment and transition into adulthood. I was only 15 at the time, but because of my extreme circumstances and maturity level, I was accepted into the program. I was the youngest teenager to be introduced to transitional living. Within three weeks, I had my own apartment.

I moved Kevin in, which was completely against the rules, but I was never one to follow the rules anyway. I was living a real grown up life and I never looked back from there. I maintained school, but because of the situation with Tide Tomas and the excessive threats and fights, I ended up leaving Eastmoor and going back to the school district I went to in middle school. Although Tide Tomas got away with what he did to me, I heard later he was caught up in some other inappropriate situations. I'm still waiting on my apology from my peers and their parents.

He Said

Chapter 6:
Inter-Smitten

 After graduation, life seemed to slow down socially, which was far from what I imagined. I was a year into my "life plan" and my intentions to join the military were getting too close for comfort. I still lived at home and I didn't see any reason to mess up a good thing. My mom didn't bother me and I came and went as I pleased with no problems. The basement was my official first apartment. All it needed was a kitchen and an entrance door. I was still working in the mall, but now I had two full time jobs and one part time job. My grandma always said, "A man who don't work, don't eat." I liked to eat.

 I tried my hand in getting money the fast way, but the consequences were too great for me so I just stuck to the legal way. It was slow, but it assured my freedom. Working in the mall was like a small community. I would get the tightest hook up on clothes, sneakers and food. It was also a good way to meet new women. I attracted a lot of ladies, but it always seemed to end up going nowhere. I'd always liked a big butt and nice feet. The female anatomy altogether was intriguing. I liked having a PYT around and it didn't matter to me too much whether something happened or not.

Because I had multiple jobs within the same mall, oftentimes I would be there from the time it opened until it closed. Over a short period of time, I got to know a lot of people fairly quickly. I began to gain a reputation because a lot of women would come in and out of my stores to come see me. I seemed enigmatic to many girls and I wasn't in their face like some thirsty niggas... So I attracted the masses based off of mystery alone. Occasionally Gloria would come by my jobs and make my entire day. I didn't light up for anyone like I did when she came around. The times when I thought I got over her, a mere thought would have me desperate again.

I didn't see Gloria that often during this time. She was living her life with a dude I considered "the new me." I rarely had negative feelings regarding Gloria, however, I did feel like she pulled the wool over my eyes for breaking up with me because I smoked weed and come to find out her new nigga was a whole Ganjapreneur. I didn't know all of the details of their relationship, but I figured if she was coming to see me, Mr. Stoner Boy must not be doing what he was supposed to.

I never gave up on the idea of Gloria and I being together. She was younger than me. Maybe she needed some time to figure things out. I lived a fast life so all the things she was just experiencing, I had already done years prior. I knew I would always be there for her and the moment she realized I was all in, I figured she would come running back. I had a bad habit of not speaking up when it came to her. When it came to matters of the heart, I had learned to keep my feelings to myself. Wearing my heart on my sleeve only got me hurt. But not speaking up got me left behind. Until I could get the nerve to be bold with my feelings, I kept myself busy entertaining faux relationships.

In October of 2000, I started dating Abe's sister who was nine years older than me. Jayla. She was a light-skinned, long-haired chick with a nice butt, thick thighs, and a boob tattoo. I'd met her in the 9th grade and I thought she was cute, but never thought about it more than that. She was Abe's sister, so technically she was off limits. She was every hood nigga's fantasy. She was aggressive too. She had been throwing hints at me for months and I was not catching them. Her baby's father was one of the biggest hitters in Columbus. She could have any dope boy of her dreams and there I was working at the mall and she was checking for me. That's how I knew I had the juice.

Before we started dating, Jayla had invited me and the fellas over to eat and hang out at her place. At this time I was catching all the hints she was throwing, so much so that I had my mind made up that we were going to close out the evening with a nightcap. Together. Alone. Naked.

We ended up playing Spades and conveniently Jayla was my partner. She started being a little energetic under the table and there really was no denying what was happening now. It started getting late and everyone was getting ready to leave. I was still sitting at the table waiting to see if she was going to keep that same energy after the game. I could tell Abe got curious because he asked me if I was leaving and stood between me and Jayla. I told him I drank a little too much and that I was going to chill for a minute. In the greatest cock block moment of our friendship, he dumped Trey on me and told me to take him home, even though they were roommates and were going to the same place. I didn't want to try and think of a reason why I couldn't do it, so I obliged. As Abe left I sat there for a few minutes talking to Jayla and Trey. I considered sending Trey on a wild goose chase to buy some time with Jayla, but he didn't have licences and he was a terrible driver, so I figured that my night was over at that point.

I signaled for Trey to head out so we could go. As I was saying bye to Jayla, she hugged me and wrapped her arms around my neck, resting her hands behind my ears and whispered in my ear slowly and told me to take her car. I told her I drove and before I could get the rest of my sentence out, she put her finger over my lips and said, "So I know that you'll come back."

I dropped Trey off on the corner of where his place was and kept going. When I arrived back at her house, she was sitting on the couch waiting on me with less clothes on than I remember her having before I left. I could see her through the screen door as I pulled up. She was posed in a ghetto swan position that was pleasing to the eye. I walked inside, took a good look and slid down next to her. We

95

started kissing and we went at it all night. We woke up and had another round before the sun came up.

After that night, we spent practically every night together, but we kept our relationship on the low for as long as we could. Abe eventually found out and he threatened to deaden our friendship over it. Even though I felt like he was overreacting, the first rule of bro code is "bros over hoes," so I told Abe I would break it off with Jayla. Secretly I kept seeing her a while after that, but in the end, our relationship didn't last because she wanted more than I was willing to give. She wanted me to move in and marry her.

Pause. I liked her. The sex was good, but I wasn't in love with her. The thoughts of marriage scared me. I only pictured myself with one person in that way and I wasn't willing to alter my imagination to fit Jayla in.

Being with Jayla made me miss intimacy and friendship. I'd often envision what it would be like to make love to Gloria. Sex was never something that was pressing between us. I just enjoyed being around her and talking. I reached back to one of my lady friends that I was cool with in high school, Denise. I started hanging out with her more regularly a few months after I stopped talking to Jayla. Trey actually introduced us when I was in the 10th grade. He thought that she would be perfect for me when he met her. I normally don't take referrals from Trey, but in this case he didn't do too bad. Denise was biracial and had a caramel skin complexion. She was really pretty and the dopest thing about her was that she was like one of the fellas. Back then, we got along great and we used to talk on the phone for hours. In high school, we wouldn't see each other that often because I stayed on the east side and she lived on the north side, and neither one of us was driving at the time. We liked each other, but nothing ever happened between us because she always had a boyfriend.

One night I thought about her and randomly called her. She invited me out drinking with some of her friends. I didn't think much would come of it. She was always attached, but I thought it would be worth my time to reunite with her. I got to the bar and realized that I had some catching up to do as they had been there drinking for awhile. They say that alcohol brings out the truth and in the midst of laughing and libations, Denise confessed that she's always liked me and didn't remember why things didn't progress between us. She proclaimed in front of all her friends that I was a real one and she wasn't going to let me slip away again.

I called Denise the next day to ask her about her drunk rant the night before. I reminded her that the reason nothing ever happened between us in high school was because of Spud, her unusually buff boyfriend. She claimed she and Spud were done, and had been for over a year, and in the same breath asked if I wanted to come by her house and catch up. Without hesitation, I agreed.

When I got to her place, we sat and talked for hours, well into the night. I forgot how comfortable she made me feel. Talking to her was like talking to one of my boys. She told me she used to think about me and would wonder what I was doing during the periods of time that we were not in communication. She said that she thought I was a pretty boy when we first met and that she used to put on this lipgloss called Candy Kisses whenever I would come over, just in case I made a move. I was flattered by her intermittent thoughts of me and told her the feeling was mutual.

Denise and I were really good friends in high school which made reaching the romantic level an easy transition. We never really ended our catch up session. It just shifted to a make out session and eventually a sexcapade. After that night with Denise, for the first time since Gloria, I considered being in a relationship and thinking beyond sex. I didn't have the same feelings about Denise that I had for Gloria, but I was comfortable.

As the relationship began to deepen, I caught myself trying to fit Denise into places where only Gloria fit. I attempted to substitute Denise for the things I wanted with Gloria. In the end it was too much. I was trying to move things along too fast and she couldn't handle it. She broke up with me in a letter where she stated she wasn't woman enough to do it in person. She was over me mistakenly calling her Gloria and recounting conversations we never had, only to discover it was a conversation I shared with Gloria.

When Denise broke up with me, I felt it. I made it a habit not to get in that deep with a woman because I knew my heart was elsewhere, but because of the familiarity, I got lost in the comfort zone. We were friends, so I thought that she had more respect for me than to break up with me in letter like we were still in high school, but I guess there is no good way to break up with someone.

It took a few months, but I got over it. I tried my hand on a couple rebound girls, but nothing beyond sex. It wasn't until I had ran into Gloria in December of 2001 that I wanted to be serious with someone again.

Chapter 7:
Repeating History

Living as an adult in high school was pretty sweet. I didn't have anyone telling me what to do. I came and went as I pleased and I got to make my own rules. At times, I missed just being a teenager, but my life was never normal anyway, so I tried not to let that get me down.

I made a new set of friends in the apartment complex that I stayed in. Angel, Nicole, and Abby. I didn't trust Abby. We met by accident when I was pulling into a parking spot and she decided to walk through the spot as I was parking. Kevin was in the car with me and I was just learning to drive. As luck would have it, he got a good look at her more-than-averaged-size ass. She certainly got his attention, and I got hers. She got bumped with my car that day.

She and I became cool that summer. I was going into my senior year and experience made me become less fearful of what this world had for me. I turned 17 and I just knew I was grown.

I finally got my license after three tries. Ironically my last attempt was in the biggest car I had ever driven. My most memorable moments in my first year of driving were picking up my little cousin, Leslie, and us blasting Trina in my 1991 Geo Storm. Leslie was only 11, but she was one of my best friends. My grandma took care of her and she was the closest thing I had to a sister. She helped me play many phone games with Kevin back in the chasing stage. I owed a lot to her.

Being in a relationship with Kevin wasn't what I imagined it to be. We fought a lot and he was gone often. I was bored and didn't feel loved. When I felt lonely, I called Derric. He always made me feel special and gave me the attention I needed. I thought about a life with him, but I quickly shut all those thoughts out because of the fear of leaving everything Kevin and I had built. I didn't come that far for nothing.

Kevin and I took a break for a while during the winter of 2001. We hit a roadblock in our relationship where the only thing left to do was get married and he wasn't ready for that life. I told him he couldn't shack up with me any longer if I wasn't wifey material. With advice from his mother, he moved back in with her. In the back of my mind, I knew he would come to his senses and decide to marry me; it was only a matter of time.

During our break, Derric and I became more familiar. I would go to the mall just to pass by the store he worked in. He would always greet me with a big hug and smile. It almost felt like every time he'd see me it was the first time in years, even if only a few days had gone by. I told him I missed him and we needed to spend some more time together, and right away, we seemed to pick up right where we left off two years prior.

He was gentle with me; I knew he was into me more than I was into him, and I can't say I didn't take advantage of that. He looked at me different from any other guy, and made me feel like there was no other girl on this earth that could compare.

Derric and I had sex for the first time on Valentine's Day 2002. It was a Thursday, the night before I had to get a major surgery. I stayed the night at his house so he could drop me off at the hospital the next morning. That night wasn't planned; it just happened. Our energy connected in a way I had never experienced before with anyone else. He took his time and we made love that night. He had never told me he loved me before, but I felt like this had to be how Cliff felt about Claire; that Huxtable love was undeniable.

Derric and I were going steady for two months straight before I began to miss Kevin. I missed the time we put in and the idea of our future. I met Kevin at the mall a few times during our break up. We talked for hours at length about the woulda, coulda, shouldas. I caught myself staring at the beauty mark he had on the right side of his face. He was so damn fine, and in my head, I immediately forgave him for all his past wrongs. I knew our future kids would be models and having cute kids was on the top of my priority list.

The last time I met with Kevin, I went home and flirted with the idea of him coming back. I got lost in my thoughts and almost forgot I had company. I had a few friends over to my apartment about to watch the R. Kelly piss tape. This was the most exciting scandal going on at the time and I made sure I had access to the exclusive footage. Right when the alleged pedophile started sprinkling golden showers, there was a loud bang at my door. I didn't know what to expect, but it sounded like the police were trying to bust through. I immediately took the tape out of my VCR and hid it under the couch, just in case. I peeked out of the window, and it was Kevin, bleeding from his shoulder to his leg.

I quickly unlocked the door and let him in. He told me he fell off his motorcycle, attempting to do donuts in the snow, and the bike ran over him and burnt his entire left side. I was panicked, but I jumped into action. He didn't want to go to the hospital so I did my best to clean him up. During this time, I knew for sure I wanted to move forward with Kevin. I imagined something worse happening, and couldn't live with myself if we weren't on good terms. I could tell he was ready to come back home, otherwise he would have gone to his mom's house for help. The real question was, was he ready to put a ring on it?

Kevin moved back into my apartment shortly after his accident. I needed to figure out how to break the news to Derric.

My prom was rapidly approaching. Derric and I had talked about it many times, but I couldn't see myself going with anyone but Kevin, especially since we were back together. It would be pretty hard to sneak a whole other guy to prom without Kevin noticing. I knew I needed to tell Derric about Kevin moving back in, but I didn't know how to break it off with Derric for the second time. I needed to find another reason to take the fault off me. I went as far as trying to hook him up with Abby's ho ass. Maybe she could distract him for a while and I could chalk it up as him having wandering eyes.

The moment came after we made love for the second time. He was headed to drop me off at my apartment while I was contemplating ways to sabotage our situation. I'm assuming he felt the sudden withdrawal and decided to shoot his shot. When we pulled up to my apartment, he grabbed my hand and told me he wanted to make "us" official again. He told me he knew about Kevin moving back, but he wasn't mad and he understood. I just needed to make a decision.

I didn't know what to say. I was a little scared that he was so calm about Kevin moving back. Then I got mad. If he knew that whole time and didn't say anything, why not just play this role then? Derric and I spent two straight months together. He got everything: my time, my attention, and my goodies. Most guys would be satisfied with that, but he always wanted more. I was so worked up, I convinced myself that he was selfish and allowed that to be my exit.

He Said

Chapter 7:
Repeating History

I'd bumped into Gloria and her friend, Abby, at the mall around Christmas 2001. It had been awhile since I had seen her and my first thought was that she looked beautiful. She'd come up to the store where I worked every so often and check on me. I'd always look forward to those meetings.

I found out through conversation that she and Kevin had broken up, so I took this as my chance to get her back. Before this, she would call me at least once a week, crying and upset, telling me how horrible this nigga Kevin was, and I couldn't understand why she didn't just leave. Why she wouldn't let me treat her how she deserved to be treated? Why did she settle for the bullshit? I was her fall back guy. An option, but not her first choice. I was someone to keep around to make her feel good when the guy she really wanted wasn't living up to what she had hoped. However, at that time, while I was in the midst of it, all I could think about was this was my chance to make her mine again.

During the time we were together, I was happy even though there were also plenty of hurtful situations that occurred with our second time around, which I just couldn't understand. Gloria played games, but I was being 100% serious with her. It became frustrating when she would tell me things like, "Abby likes you," tempting me to give her friend a chance because she thought we might get along better. Even the times we were out together on a date, she would seem disrespectful and flirt with other guys. Plenty of times I wanted to shake the shit out of her, like, "What the fuck is wrong with you!? Why would you disrespect me like that?" But I didn't say anything because I was too afraid that she would leave me again. I didn't want to do anything that I thought would upset her, even if that meant standing up for myself.

We had a special night on Valentine's Day of '02. I still lived with my mom in the basement, but she was out of town that whole week, so I had the house to myself. I wanted to make love to Gloria all night. I wanted to hold her and tell her I didn't want to live another day without her. I wanted her to know she was everything to me and more.

I spent a lot of time wishing I could be the person that I was when I was around other girls. I was mad at myself for being nervous and timid around her, but she really brought out something different in me. It felt good, but I didn't feel like I was in control. I felt like I was a puppet and my emotions had their hand up my ass controlling my every move. Most of the time, I didn't think the person I was was good enough for her. That fear of rejection kept me in bondage. We shared an intimate moment that night, but I failed to tell her how I felt.

I wanted Gloria to be just as crazy about me as she was for Kevin. I couldn't figure out what he had that I didn't, but I was determined to figure it out. Toward the end of our time spent together that spring, my cousin BJ told me that Gloria and Kevin were getting back together, and asked me did I know about it? Of course I didn't and I wondered how he knew that information before I did. But I just simply answered no.

I didn't say anything to Gloria about it right away; I just watched her movements. I noticed she didn't invite me over to her apartment anymore or have me drop her off in front of her building. She always seemed to have something on her mind and wasn't as affectionate. She spent the night at my place a second time and I could tell her mind was somewhere else. We had sex that night. It was different than the first time.

The next morning I asked her about Kevin on the way back to her apartment. She seemed surprised that I knew, but admitted he moved back in and they were getting back together. To be honest, that shit brought tears to my eyes. She told me I should be happy because I got everything but the title. She was playing with my feelings, but I still couldn't bring myself to be hateful toward her. I didn't get everything that I wanted because I wanted the title. The title was everything.

She got out of the car angry. Everything happened so fast that I was sure this was entirely my fault. I needed her to hear me, but no matter what I said, she had her mind made up. Even though I was angry with her, I watched her walk to her door to make sure that she got inside safely. I pulled off reliving that moment in my head on the way to Abe's house. Why wasn't I good enough to be loved? Why couldn't I be her main attraction? I felt rejected on so many levels, but I kept allowing her to let me down everytime. I thought it was better to have her and keep losing her, than to never have her at all.

A week went by and per usual, Kevin and Gloria split up. We were back "together" hanging out again in no time.

The day I realized that I was in love with Gloria hit me like a ton of bricks. I mentioned to her that I wanted to get my tongue pierced, which she seemed excited about. She told me if I really wanted to do it, she would pay for it. We both agreed and did it without hesitation.

After the procedure was completed, my tongue felt like it weighed 1,000 lbs and the pain was indescribable. Without even asking, she made two stops. The first was to Wendy's to get a cup of ice and the second was at a gas station for some aspirin. When we arrived at the gas station, Gloria got out of the car to get the medication. I was sitting in the passenger seat of my car watching her walk to the door. I was thinking about how she was taking care of me. Even though this was a small thing, she was still making sure that I was okay.

I never had anyone outside of my mom or grandma look after me in that way before. I also thought about how I felt when I was around her and how I felt when I didn't have her. I knew right then that what I had been feeling this whole time was love. I was in love with her and I immediately got scared because I knew I had to tell her, but I was afraid that she wouldn't feel the same.

When she got back into the car, I was all smiles. Love will make you smile for every reason or for no reason at all. When we parted ways that day, I felt good, but I also felt regret not telling her about my love revelation right away. It was still kind of early, so I headed to Abe's to see what was up for the night.

After about an hour of hanging with Abe, I worked up the nerve to tell Gloria how I felt. With excitement, I decided to call her to pour out my heart. When Gloria answered, she sounded a little upset. I never got a chance to tell her anything before she told me that she was not able to talk to me anymore because she was getting back together with Kevin. I was speechless, but it didn't matter. She had hung up before I could even formulate a thought. She made her decision and I guess somewhere deep down inside, I knew she would never choose me. I was always an option to Gloria, but never her priority.

In the days after that last disappointment, I fell into a slump. I really didn't know what to do. I called off work for a few days to clear my head. When I returned, all I could think about was how my two-year plan deadline was approaching and I needed to start making some bigger moves.

All of the sudden, Abby walked in. I was surprised to see her because she and Gloria were usually together. She told me they had fallen out for some reason so that's why she had not been around. Abby noticed my demeanor and asked me what was wrong since I looked visibly upset. I told her that Gloria and I were no longer talking because she was getting back with Kevin. Abby basically said that she knew that Gloria was going to do that and offered her condolences.

She wanted to know what time I was getting off work and invited me to her apartment because it looked like I needed someone to talk to. I felt like she wanted something more from me than to just talk, but I told her that I would let her know. We didn't exchange numbers, but Abby said she would call me at my job a little later to see whether I was going to come over. I seriously thought about having sex with Abby that night to get back at Gloria for all the bullshit she took me through. Besides, this is what she wanted. She gave us her blessing. When Abby called, I agreed to come over.

When I arrived at Abby's apartment, she greeted me with a hug and invited me in. The hug was extra. She made sure to press her breasts up against my chest and wiggle them in a way that would get my attention. To my surprise, we sat across from each other and actually talked. I poured my heart out, and at the end of the conversation, I think we both understood that my heart belonged to Gloria. I cared about Gloria too much to mess around with her friend.

However, I liked Abby, and surprisingly, she was there for me regardless of her original intention. I actually felt better when I left her house. We exchanged numbers and ended up becoming friends. This was still probably a form of betrayal, but at the time I felt like Gloria couldn't really be mad since she chose Kevin. Abby and I began to hang out on a regular basis and even though we got along great and had fun together, all I could think about was Gloria.

Kevin was cheating on Gloria. She suspected it and I saw and heard things around town that indicated he wasn't the most faithful. I was out with Abby one day when we saw Kevin with a girl Gloria and I went to high school with, coming out of a fast food place. He had a big smile on his face while opening the car door for her.

All I could do was shake my head. Why would Gloria choose this guy over me? He didn't even respect her, I thought to myself. I wanted to tell her that I saw her "man" out with another girl, but I knew it would just come off jealous. I wanted to tell her that he didn't love her like I did. She made me want things that I had never wanted before. I wanted to marry her and have babies, I wanted a house in the suburbs, I wanted to be her husband, and I wanted to cherish her and let her know that she was special.

116

Despite all my effortless hopes and dreams, she ended up marrying Kevin later that year and had his baby the next year. This nigga stole my life and there was nothing I could do about it. I joined the Air Force in 2003 before her child was born. I needed to leave Columbus and all of the painful memories behind me.

Chapter 8:
Holy Crap

As far back as I can remember, I've always had some affiliation with church. My grandma and grandpa would make sure my cousins and I didn't miss a day in attendance. The dreadfully long hours every Sunday spilled over to the week for Bible study, missionary meetings, usher board meetings, choir rehearsals and night services. All that church, but still no God. I had no idea about religion or faith, all I knew was I had better be dressed like Jesus was coming back any day.

As a young child, I despised church. I didn't understand what the pastor was fussing about. I paid more attention to the fact that he was sounding like he was going into an asthmatic attack than what he was actually saying. Even children's church was confusing. Oftentimes, I stared off into space, thinking about other things, wishing someone would save me from this holy prison. I would always hear the pastor say, "Jesus *haaa*, loves you *ha haaaa*, and He *HAA,* will neva leave you. *Haaa shabock.*" Jesus loves me? Those words stuck with me, as I questioned every ounce of the meaning. At five years old, my definition of love was being touched inappropriately by men who should have been role models. I didn't know much about this Jesus, but I knew if He never left me, I could find solace in my adversities.

I knew at a young age I was different. Things happened to me that didn't seem to happen to anyone else. I saw things other people couldn't see; I knew things other people didn't know. Because I considered myself fatherless, I was always open. I wanted to identify with something or someone, which gave me opportunities to explore many things. I went from wanting to be Punky Brewster, to believing Jim Carrey was my real father.

I was nine years old when my mother told me I had an identity crisis. She felt like I talked too "white" and told me I needed help. I remember the look of disgust on her face when she glared her bloodshot eyes on my favorite Bart Simpson sweater. She hated the sight of me. I couldn't understand why. This woman who birthed me couldn't stand my presence for longer than five minutes before she began to tear me down.

My mother did a lot of things a young child should never see. But what stood out most was her constant effort to pray and read the Bible. There were many times when my mom came in from a night of getting high and the first thing she would do is drop to her knees and cry out to God. I would watch her through the opening of the skeleton key hole on the door. Sometimes she would spend hours just pleading with God.

I'd open her Bible, barely able to read, but the array of colorful markers that outlined her favorite passages drew my attention. I began emulating my mother's actions with prayer. Oftentimes I didn't know how to articulate what I needed, but I knew He would never leave me and that He could see the same things I could see. I prayed about the lottery a lot. I asked God if we could win the lottery because I correlated wealth with happiness. I thought if we had a lot of money, my mom would stop doing drugs and marry someone who would be my father and we could live around a lot of white people. That was my idea of success.

I prayed that same prayer for years, and then I just stopped. My prayer life was non-existent again until my teenage years.

He Said

Chapter 8:
Holy Crap

Growing up in a black household, church was damn near mandatory. One thing I can say about my community is we had no problem reverencing God, and made it a point to tell people, "God is good... All the time, and all the time, God is good." Coming from a Baptist background, getting up early every Sunday putting on a suit, going to Sunday School before service, was protocol. Even growing up with that being all I knew, I still despised it. It felt more like a punishment than a revival. I had a hard time praying to a God that would allow my family to be broken and my father to leave. That's where my community and I went our separate ways. I didn't feel like God was always good to me. I didn't like being a child even as a child. I hated the idea of someone else making decisions for me.

During church services I would draw. My mind would wander and I always found solace in creating my own picture. However, there were times where I was actually paying attention. I could never connect to what was being said. There were things that never really made sense to me, but it never bothered me enough to cross check. By the time I was in my teens, my mother had stopped going to church on the regular and I was okay with it to say the least.

As I got older, I began questioning everything. I found tenacity to debrief those things that had been fed to me all those years growing up in the Baptist church. And although I believed in education, both formal and self-taught, just like school didn't teach me everything, neither did the church. I found humor in asking my fellow black folks why they were Christians. Most said it was because they believe in God. Oddly enough, you can believe in God and not be a Christian. So the real answer was that most of them didn't know.

Through my curiosity, I spent some time studying religion, only to learn slaves were taught Christianity by the slave master. It was used as a weapon to keep slaves in check. A weapon that captured people and took them away from their homeland, held them against their will and forced them to do manual labor without compensation. I always wondered if black people had never been slaves, would we even be Christians. I didn't believe religion was inherently evil, but the act was perpetrated by evil men. Understanding that made it even harder for me to participate.

Who hurt you? Was the question I was asked most frequently when it came to my religious beliefs. And my answer would be, *"Where should I start?"* From having a father who emotionally damaged my mom, mentally ruined me, and physically abused himself... that should be enough to understand my hesitation. I'd hear stories about little boys being touched by Catholic pastors and I would just shake my head. The people we are taught to trust first end up hurting us the most. I was not atheist, but I didn't want to be categorized by religion. I believed in God, a higher power, and Jesus. I didn't indulge in the Bible well enough to know if I agreed with everything, but I also didn't seek validation in other denominations or religions. Staying ignorant, but believing there was a God, seemed the safest.

She Said

Chapter 9:
He loves me; he loves me not

On September 15, 2002, I became Mrs. Kevin Dottson. Everything happened so fast. One minute I was at my senior prom, the next I was on one knee proposing to Kevin. I had been very patient with waiting on him to pop the question, so I decided to take things into my own hands. I had acquired some money from my grandpa, which was supposed to be for car repairs on a car he gave me for graduation. Little did he know that Kevin had bought me another car and I had used the repair money to buy Kevin a wedding ring. Of course, that secret didn't stay in the bag long. My mom told my grandpa what I did and he became so furious, he never showed up to my wedding, let alone walked me down the aisle.

The wedding was a mess. It rained that day, and it was supposed to be an outside wedding in the Park of Roses. I had no back up plan for inclement weather, so we had to call all of the guests and tell them to just go to the reception location. Somehow my family threw together a small ceremony. It came together enough to not be a laughing stock. We ran out of food and there was no order of service or playlist for the DJ; we were just winging it. I had turned 18 three weeks prior to the wedding and I was afraid to drink the champagne when we toasted. I felt like a little kid at a bar.

This is what I had dreamed of all my life, being a wife and having someone love me unconditionally and never leave me. I wanted to be a mother and show my mom what it looked like to love a child. I wanted all the things that the American dream had to offer, and I planned my life accordingly. But there were some things that I didn't plan for.

During our honeymoon in Florida, I found out Kevin was cheating on me. I confronted him immediately after a phone call that I eavesdropped on. He was having a conversation with a girl he hooked up with on one of his many trips to "see his dad" in California. He denied cheating on me, but I knew better. The flight home was silent. I was conjuring up my plan to catch him in the act. I had to be strategic because he was never going to admit to it and now that he knew I was on to him, he was more careful.

The day we got back from our honeymoon, he had a flight planned to Vegas the next day without me. When he left, I went through all of his things trying to find some clues of infidelity. I didn't find anything concrete, except a handwritten phone number in one of his jean jacket with the name: *Shyanne*. The area code was not familiar, so I called the operator to find out what location matched with a 760 area code. Sure enough, it was some city in California.

I had quickly ran to the shoe box where I kept all of our bills. I was looking for an itemized phone bill. I wanted to see how many times this California number showed up on Kevins line.

Thirty-two… That number rang in my head like an echo in the Grand Canyon. This nigga talked to this whore 32 times in ONE month? I was livid, and I could feel the blood rushing to my face and my heart beating wildly. It was 1 am EST and I needed to confront Kevin right then and there.

I called his phone 23 times with no answer. I left 12 messages and I finally decided to break into his voicemail. At first, my goal was to see if he left my messages unheard, or if he was listening to them and ignoring me. I would be able to tell by the amount of new messages he received. He had 13 new messages, indicating he didn't listen to my messages yet and someone else had left him a new message also. I took it upon myself to skip through all of my messages to get to that one mystery voicemail. I was anxious and scared as to what I might hear, but I needed to deal with it head on. As I got to the new message, the robot lady seemed to take her time, and then I heard a girl's voice say, *"Hey baby, I lost you. Call me back, I'm in front of MGM with Ce-Ce."* Who the fuck was Ce-Ce? And what the hell was the MGM? And who in the entire fuck was she calling baby? I instantly got sick.

That was just the first of many infidelities, but instead of leaving the marriage, I stayed and gathered information. Information that I suppose I would have used for a big reveal. When Kevin thought I was getting close to leaving, he would hand me a stack of money and tell me to go shopping. Retail therapy kept us together for some time.

But I needed more; I needed to be loved and paid attention to. Not money.

I thought about Derric every time I found out something new about Kevin. I wondered what my life would have been like if I'd never broken up with him for Kevin. I wondered if we would still be together or if he would have ever cheated on me. I needed to talk to him, but I couldn't face him after I got married to the very guy I dumped him for. He probably hated the very sound of my voice.

A few months after our honeymoon, I found out I was pregnant. I couldn't very well leave at that time, otherwise I would become everything I worked so hard to avoid. I didn't want to become a statistic and I didn't want to have a "baby daddy." I wanted to be a wife, not a single mother on welfare; I wanted the family I was robbed of as a child. I knew for sure Derric would never speak to me again, knowing I was pregnant with Kevin's baby. This was the ultimate betrayal.

Our son was born July 23, 2003 at 1:27 am. Damn Leo; I tried hard to push him out before midnight, but he was stubborn and came when he was ready–dominate Leo trait. His father named him after himself and his grandfather John. He put the two names together to form a name that most employers would avoid and all of his teachers would indubitably mispronounce: Ka'John. I never agreed to that name prior to him signing the birth certificate. I'd always felt it was safe to have a "white name" just to have a chance at life.

Kevin was a better father than he was a husband. He took pride in his son and took him everywhere he went. Before Ka'John was one, Kevin made sure they were twins and had matching everything. He had more Jordans than he had diapers. I loved how much he loved his son and I admired the passion he had to be a good father. I wish I could say I felt the same love towards me, but I didn't. Not only that, but I was coming into womanhood and things looked different to me. I was a mother, so my tolerance for certain things was conflicting.

I didn't like how Kevin wore his pants low or how big his clothes were. I wasn't attracted to that anymore and I was starting to feel more like his mother than his wife. I wanted to join a church and learn more about God and the

Bible. Even though I didn't grow up with the knowledge of the Word, I somehow felt connected, but I didn't know how to make it official. I believed getting back to church as an adult would answer some daunting childhood questions. However, Kevin wouldn't budge. He wasn't raised that way and didn't believe we needed to go to church in order to believe in God. I would find myself visiting churches alone, crying amongst the people because I felt the pastor was talking directly to me and giving me clues to get out of my marriage.

I was too afraid to stand on my own. I didn't want people to say, "I told you so," and most of all, I didn't want to face the failures that could lie ahead. I was more worried about what people would think than I was with my own health and happiness. I decided to take the cowardly approach in order to get out. I would set it up to make it seem like I was a victim of adultery. I already had all of the evidence regarding his infidelites. All I needed was a plan.

I set Kevin up to cheat on me. I hired one of my friends, who happened to be a woman of loose character, to seduce him, and he fell right into the trap. I didn't waste any time confronting him. As soon as he got home from the dirty act, I was waiting. In an effort to cut the bullshit, I had the loose friend walk in shortly after to expose the details. He was speechless. Honestly, I regretted it right after she said they were walking in the hotel room. I was sick with dangerous emotions and all I could do was scream.

My son was six months when his dad and I separated. I moved into my first apartment as a single adult and had to get a real job to support my son. I felt lonely and lost, but at the same time I was excited about the opportunity to live my best life and sow my royal oats. A lot of my teenage years and young adult years were spent chasing after Kevin, so at that point, I got a chance to see where my new life would take me.

I got my first management job at Man Alive, which was an urban clothing store in the mall. I was a co-manager to the assistant manager. I was part of an all woman, young and black management team. I would want to count that trio as a black girl magic moment, but it was nothing short of ratchet. We would fight all of the time, compete for attention and sabotage each other's jobs constantly. I was the least favorite, and most of the time the other two managers would band together to attempt to intimidate me. I had more to lose. I was the only one out of us three that had a child and lived on my own, so I could care less about the pettiness. I needed a paycheck.

Working at the mall, I met a lot of people, especially with working in an urban clothing store; we brought all the boys to the yard. One day I was working on merchandising and changing the mannequins, when Derric walked in. He walked right past me and started looking at one of the male exhibits I had just dressed in a Rock-A-Wear army fatigue outfit. As he stood there, I began to reminisce on how he touched me and how gentle he always was with me, which put a huge smile on my face. I hadn't seen him for two years and it looked like the military had done his body good.

I was excited to see him, but nervous about his reaction. I didn't know if he would receive me or reject me, and he was well within his right to never speak to me again. I decided to shoot my shot. I walked right up to him and gave him a hug. Surprisingly he embraced me like there was never any issue between us. I felt something from him that I never felt with Kevin. I was open to receive more of whatever he was willing to give me at this point in my life.

I was hoping Derric wasn't attached. He left for the military shortly after I got married and was stationed out of New Mexico, so it was likely he could have met someone. Chicks love a man in uniform.

I decided not to ask and just enjoy him. He was home for a few months and I wanted to make sure we spent as much time together as possible. We seemed to pick up right where we left off and I began to look at him in a whole new light. I wasn't afraid anymore to consider him in my future. In fact, I liked that idea. I gave him a key to my apartment so he could come and go as he pleased while I was at work. We really jumped into a full adult relationship and worked well together. We made love every chance we had with no regard to any consequences. I trusted him and I knew he would never put me in any compromising situations.

It came time to introduce Derric to Ka'John. This was one of the scariest moments I've experienced. Ka'John had never been around another man other than his father, grandfather, and uncles. Also, this was a child conceived after I decided to leave Derric behind. I was worried about him rejecting my son out of bitterness.

While Derric was friendly to Ka'John, I could tell he was slightly uncomfortable. He was at least overthinking it because there were times he seemed to look right past the baby and just be frozen. I didn't press the issue and I tried to limit the time I had Ka'John around Derric so it didn't bring back any hurtful memories.

July 22, 2014. One day before my son's first birthday, Derric and I were at his mom's house on the swinging chair in the backyard, recounting memories, when I heard him suddenly say, "I love you." I stopped the swing and asked him to repeat what I'd thought I heard. He looked at me nervously and said it again. I was shocked that we went from talking about high school orientation to him abruptly confessing his love. My first reaction was, *"Really?"* I couldn't understand how he could love me past all of the rejections. But I knew if he loved me in spite of the hurt, that I had a good thing. I told him I loved him too. At that time, I didn't understand the magnitude of his love, but I knew I never been cared for so much by anyone, and I loved him for loving me unconditionally.

As we went in for the kiss to seal our newly found love, I received a phone call on my cell. It was my grandfather calling; I hadn't spoken to him in months. Ever since he refused to come to my wedding, I had had no words for him. I let the phone ring to voicemail and continued making out with Derric. The phone rang again, which was odd, because he had never called me back to back before. This time I decided to answer. It was his daughter-in-law, Charlotte. I thought it was strange, her calling me from my grandfather's phone, but immediately after hearing her voice, I knew something was terribly wrong.

My grandfather had suffered a heart attack and died. I didn't get to say goodbye or even settle our differences before he left this earth. I instantly fell to the ground and laid prostrate in an effort to bring him back through my pleas. Derric's mother ran out to comfort me, but all I wanted to do was sink as far into the ground as possible. Derric seemed overwhelmed with the responsibility of catering to my emotional meltdown, and although we had just exchanged love vows, something in me died for him when he couldn't be what I needed him to be in that moment.

The next few weeks following my grandfather's passing, I spent a lot of time writing and staying to myself. Many people reached out and offered their condolences and Kevin seemed to lead the pack. He sent me flowers and cards, calling often to check on me. My heart was beginning to soften back up for him, and with me losing family that was so close to me, I began to reconsider the idea of my family with Kevin and our son.

Derric needed to go back to New Mexico, and at that point, I was ready to have some time between us. I needed to clear my mind and reevaluate my emotions. My birthday normally was a pretty big deal to me, but I just stayed home and wallowed. Ever since freshman year in high school, Derric had never missed an opportunity to acknowledge my birthday. Even when we weren't speaking, or when I broke up with him countless times, he still found it in his heart to send me a card or flowers every year. If I could count on anything, I could count on him to make me smile every August 2nd.

The night before Derric was scheduled to leave, I was home alone listening to Mary J Blige, in my feelings about love and life, when I received a knock on the door. It was Kevin. I hadn't been expecting him, but I wasn't disappointed to see him. He was saying and doing all the right things I needed in my life at that moment. He came in and gently touched the side of my face and told me he was there for me. Somehow not too long after that we were both down to our underwear.

As soon as things escalated, there was a loud knock at the door. I was so completely thrown off by Kevin that I forgot that Derric was coming by for his last night in town. Kevin looked at me aggressively and asked, "Who the fuck is that?"

I tried to act like I didn't know who would be knocking at my door at that time of night. But I was also praying Derric didn't use his key and catch us in this uncomfortable situation.

Kevin decided to take matters in his own hands and muscled his way to the door with only his boxers on. He swung open the door to see two dozen roses staring at him right in his face. He angrily asked, "Who the fuck are you?" It was Derric behind those beautifully arranged roses, and I was cowardly peeking around my bedroom door, waiting for a fight to break out. What happened next was worse.

Derric dropped the flowers, caught my eye, shook his head and walked away. He didn't stay and get confrontational; he didn't show any emotion. I didn't even get so much as a "fuck you." Perhaps he was tired of the bullshit, but the silence killed me more than any weapon could.

Kevin left in a hurry that night in an attempt to catch up with Derric. He acted as if Derric challenged him to a street fight, but I understand Kevin's pride was on the line. He wasn't mature enough to have a civilized conversation, so his way of dealing with the situation was to flex his muscles. I tried to call Derric right after he drove off, but the phone just went to voicemail. As I picked up the broken flowers, a note from Derric fell out. The front of the card said, *"831."* On the back of the card read, "Eight letters, three words, one meaning." He was reinforcing the way he said he had always felt for me. Kevin didn't return that night or even the weeks following. Neither one of them would answer my calls and I began to feel like I was reaping all of the bad things I sowed, especially toward Derric.

On September 2, 2004, I found out I was pregnant again. I knew it was Derric's child and I felt angry that I had allowed myself to be in this dumbass situation. Technically I was still married and my estranged husband really wasn't speaking to me. Derric wouldn't return any of my phone calls and I was basically the poster child for every statistic I tried to fight against. I knew right away I couldn't have another child, especially out of wedlock, but technically in wedlock, with another man's child. That was a Jerry Springer episode waiting to happen.

I wasn't sure if Derric would ever speak to me again and I didn't want a sympathy relationship. I didn't want to be that girl who called the unexpecting father to tell him he was going to be a dad, in hopes that a baby would bring them back together. I also didn't want to have to face Kevin. If we were to ever get back together, another man's child would interrupt the family dynamic. He would spit on me and never look back. So I selfishly chose to abort the pregnancy and decided to not tell a single soul until it was absolutely necessary.

140

He Said

Chapter 9:
She loves me; she loves me not

November 2003, Albuquerque, New Mexico. My life in the military at that point was busy. I experienced a lot within a short amount of time and it gave me a sense of fulfillment. I saw the world from a different perspective and I had acquired certain tools I lacked as a young man. It's funny how I barely knew my father, but I was following in his footsteps rapidly. Being in the military was almost like living on a different planet. It's literally it's own world. The food was different, the duties were more pertinent, and the women were readily available.

I spent a lot of time trying to forget about Gloria. I went back to my old ways and indulged in women whenever I got the opportunity. Sex was different. I had my fun and partied, but at the end of the day, it was just sex, meaningless sex. I attempted to be in a relationship with a girl from back home right after I enlisted. I thought I was open to the idea of being married and having a family. I soon realized that idea was tailor-made for one person only. I could keep myself busy with random women, but ultimately I was only wasting their time. I wasn't ever going to marry anyone unless it was Gloria. That dreamed had died when she gave up her last name for someone else.

I wanted to hate her, but I couldn't. The very thought of her made my heart stop and my soul smile. While in the military, I picked up journaling. I wrote Gloria a letter every night for a year, as a way to self-medicate. I never sent them to her. When writing wasn't enough, I prayed. I learned the Lord's Prayer and many other Biblical verses that I spoke silently to myself to keep me encouraged. Even though I was never an outright praiser, I had a relationship with God and He knew my heart. At the time, I just wish I had known His plan.

By the summer of 2004, I hadn't seen or spoken to Gloria in two years. I kept up with some things in order to stay in the know. I was made aware when Gloria had her baby. I remember that phone call like it was yesterday. I never felt so double-crossed in my life. I kept recounting our last moments together in 2002, what I could have done differently. What if I had told her I loved her then and was more aggressive with my approach... that might have been our child instead of theirs. She might be my wife instead of Kevin's. Those thoughts constantly haunted me.

Several months after Gloria had her child, I received a letter from Abby. She sent me letters frequently, but this one was different. This letter was eight pages and I couldn't tell you what the hell it said in its entirety. The only thing that stood out was, *"Kevin is divorcing Gloria."* Common sense should've told me to leave this situation alone and move on, but something in me couldn't settle on not having her in my life. My wheels were back spinning.

I decided to take leave and go back to Columbus for my birthday to spend a few weeks in town. Abe had previously told me Gloria was working in the mall, so when I got into town, the first thing I did was call the store to see if she was there. When I called, Gloria answered the phone so I hung up. I didn't want her to know that I was coming to see her.

I was excited and a little nervous. I was with Trey and didn't mention we were going to see Gloria. I just played it casual until we came up on her store. I couldn't get in there fast enough. I walked in and acted like I didn't see her. Ironically, I stopped right in front of this army fatigue jumpsuit that was conveniently placed in the middle of the store. She walked over to me and had a big smile on her face, and said the most romantic words I'd ever heard her say, "So you goin' to act like you don't see nobody?"

I couldn't help but smile at her familiar sassiness and the refreshing friendliness in her tone. We embraced each other and I inhaled her sweet scent, which took me right back to a place where it felt like we never stopped talking.

Gloria was still married to Kevin, but they were separated. She told me that she was going to get a divorce and I wanted to believe it. Gloria had had a little boy and he was almost a year old when I returned to Columbus. I still loved her, but the fact that she had a baby with someone else was fucking me up. It was a hard pill to swallow. But I still wanted the same things. I still wanted to be with her no matter what. I felt like I had just received another chance to make this work.

We hung out the entire time I was there, which was about a month. We reached levels we never reached before which made me confident that this time our relationship would last. Gloria gave me a key to her apartment, indicating she trusted me enough to share something so personal. To me it meant loyalty. She wouldn't have given me a key if she was messing with anyone else.

I finally got the balls that summer to tell her that I loved her. I told her that I'd always loved her and that I wanted to marry her. That moment was short-lived because she received some devastating news about her grandfather. I wanted to embrace her and tell her it was going to be okay. I wanted to take all the pain she was feeling and carry it on my back for her, but I just froze.

I didn't know what was going on on the other end of the phone when she received the call, but all I knew was that my moment had been stolen from me. The moment I had been waiting more that five years for. I couldn't move I knew that I needed to go comfort Gloria and, if nothing else, just hold her, but I had too many racing thoughts. Who was delivering the information? Why did she ignore the call the first time? Why didn't she run towards me for comfort, like she always did with Kevin? Although my immediate feeling was compassion, my insecurities overshadowed everything that was reasonable.

My mother jumped right into action, came out to do what I should have done, which was comfort her silently. Then my mother walked her to the car and she drove off quickly. My mom told me Gloria's grandfather had died and I immediately felt like an ass.

After Gloria received the news of her grandfather passing, she was different. The fun-loving, quirky woman I loved seemed to be suppressed underneath the weight of the world. We spent less time together and I felt like she didn't want to be around me. I tried not to take things personally. I knew she was going through a tough time; I just didn't know how to fix it or even if I could.

I had to report back to base soon, so I wanted to make my last few days with Gloria special. She had been locking herself in her apartment for the previous week, so I wanted to surprise her with flowers and her favorite candy before my departure.

When I pulled up, her place was dark. The only light came from the reflection of her TV. I decided not to use my key because the element of surprise seemed intriguing. I knocked a few times and after the third set of knocks, the door flew open. For the first time, Kevin and I stood face to face. I didn't ask any questions. What's understood didn't need to be explained. I tossed the flowers and candy, and headed to the airport a day early.

The return to my duty station in Albuquerque was a hard thing to do under those conditions. I was in a bad place and I felt like I had lost a part of my soul. I didn't understand why I wasn't good enough for Gloria, why I was the fallback guy, and why everybody I chose to love left me in some way. I was a long way from home and I felt it. I didn't have anyone in New Mexico that I was close to at the time and so I started drinking to forget about my losses.

In an effort to forget about Gloria, I became reckless with my choice of women—anyone would do. I was at a party on base when I met a girl named Sophia. The main reason I even approached her was because I thought she was Indian. Indian girls don't usually talk to black men and I was drunk so I thought it would be a fun challenge.

When I found out that she was not Indian, but in fact, Mexican, I was a little disappointed. However, she seemed cool so I kept hanging out with her. What originally was supposed to be a quick hook up turned into an unexpected and unwanted relationship. It didn't help that I was projecting my feelings for Gloria onto her, so I thought I liked her more than I actually did.

A few months in we started having disagreement after disagreement, which turned into verbal fights. If I were in Columbus under normal circumstances, I would have been done with her immediately, but I was in Albuquerque and I was incredibly lonely. My plan was to get out of the Air Force once my enlistment was up and move to L.A. I wanted to get even further away from Columbus. I wasn't planning on telling Sophia I was leaving.

On Thanksgiving of 2004, I went to Phoenix to visit my cousin for the holidays. Before I left, Sophia found the journal I wrote in and questioned me about Gloria. I didn't feel I owed her an explanation and I was upset that she was snooping through my things. She argued with me over the phone the whole way down to Phoenix and ultimately "broke up" with me during that argument. I was relieved.

When I reached my cousin's house, I was determined to have a good time. I hadn't seen my cousin, August, in over two years so I spent some time catching up with her. August took me out to a couple clubs in Phoenix and I began to forget about my problems. I was no longer with Sophia, so I wasn't worried about going back and having to deal with some bullshit.

On my drive back to Albuquerque, Sophia called over twenty times and I chose to ignore all of her calls. I didn't want the idea of her reconsidering to even be entertained. With all my efforts to disregard her calls, she still found a way to get through. She busted through my Nextel 2-way chirp with devastating news. She was pregnant with my child.

I felt like Michael Corleone from *The Godfather: Part III*: "Just when I thought I was out, they pull me back in." I wanted kids with Gloria and that was it. If that wasn't going to happen, I didn't want kids at all. I especially didn't want kids with Sophia. I didn't even like her as a person. She had a pretty face, but some loose screws.

I had a range of emotions, none of them happy. I thought about Gloria and how my idea of our lives together was fading one disaster at a time. I thought about not wanting to be attached to Sophia, who was essentially a stranger. But overall, I knew I couldn't walk out of an innocent child's life. I would be a hypocrite if I did the very thing my father did to me. I knew I didn't want to end up like my father, so I had to step up to my responsibilities and face the consequences of my reckless actions.

I spent countless nights tossing and turning, thinking about how I ended up in a sunken place. I felt that despite all the hell Gloria took me through, she should still receive the courtesy of me telling her I got someone pregnant and not hear it from someone else.

The same morning I got the courage to tell Gloria about the pregnancy was the day my world was turned upside down with the worst news I have ever gotten. Gloria had been pregnant with my child from the time I spent in Columbus, but had gotten an abortion without my knowledge.

I was devastated. I felt like the entire world was falling apart around me. I had to deal with being rejected, but I never imagined my unborn child would have to face rejection because of me.

Chapter 10:
Dying Love

Kevin and I had been officially separated for more than a year at this point. In that year's time, I managed to lose myself, find myself and reinvent myself. I found my real father through an online people search tool and immediately flew out to Jersey to meet him.

He looked nothing like I imagined or how my mom said he was. He was a lean muscular man with dark hair and freckles and he had four kids, two of which were babies. We spent weeks trying to catch up on a lifetime. I didn't know how to address him, so I only spoke to him when he was near me so I could avoid having to call him anything. I practiced saying the word, "Dad" but it felt wrong, almost like I was cussing. Besides I hadn't officially obtained a DNA test so I didn't force something that could potentially be untrue.

I finally filed the paperwork for the divorce from Kevin and was waiting on a court date. Concurrently, I spent a lot of time trying to fit new guys in an equation that was never meant for them. I was never good at being single. There was something that I needed from a man that I couldn't get on my own, and I was determined to stay whole.

At the time, I was visiting a lot of churches, trying to find a place that felt right. I wanted desperately to be able to connect with God through the church, but I was having a hard time following what was being said, and me reading the Bible was like trying to read Braille. It was a whole other language. But I kept going and I kept inquiring and soon my chase shifted directions.

I had a few guys I was dating, but I wasn't really into. In an effort to stay busy, I had a different guy for each occasion. When I needed a buddy and a good time, to genuinely laugh, hang out and be carefree, I would call Donte.

Donte was about five feet even with stubby hands and a bald head. He was one of the funniest guys I ever met and he reminded me of someone from my childhood crew. I felt comfortable with him. I wasn't attracted to him sexually and because of his height, I never considered him a serious option.

When I needed to be wined and dined, I'd call Chaz. I wasn't quite sure what he did as a career, but I knew he would always wear tailor-fitted suits and drove the newest Benz. His condo looked like it had been professionally decorated. He had the prettiest teeth one could imagine and smiled all the time. He was a perfect gentlemen.

I stayed over at his condo a few times when we had some late nights and he would literally tuck me into his bed and sleep on his couch. He never forced sex, allowing me to choose that moment at my own pace. He didn't have to wait too long; that chivalry shit turned me on.

Chaz and I eventually began having sex frequently, always protected. Every time we had sex, I noticed the condom would slip off or break. He wasn't working with that much to bust through a condom, but at the time I didnt think too much about it, chalking it up as an accident.

I hadn't talked to Derric in more than a year. When I'd told him about the abortion, he retaliated by getting someone pregnant. I was hurt, but I couldn't blame him... although I did. With him, I wanted to have my cake and eat it too. I couldn't imagine him being on top of someone else, making love as gently as he did to me. I tried not to think of that too often, but my heart and mind would frequently fight over the hypocrisy.

Kevin spent most of our separation with his girlfriend that he broke up with for me. It was a hard pill to swallow. I felt like his heart never left her if he thought enough about her to run back.

Kevin kept his distance from me for a long time. Christmas of 2005 was approaching and Kevin seemed to be softening up to me again. He wanted to take Ka'John and me to get Christmas pictures as a "family" so our son would have something to reference to as he got older. I agreed. Neither of us knew it at the time, but these would be the last family photos we would take together.

Kevin and I continued to keep in touch on a personal level outside the connection formed by having our son. I could tell he missed our family dynamic and I would be remiss if I said I didn't feel the same. I just couldn't get the idea of him sleeping with his ex and my hoe friend out of my head. It certainly prolonged the idea of us working out our marriage.

In the meantime, I continued to hang out with Donte and Chaz. I could talk to Chaz about my separation and conflicting feelings and he would be a shoulder for me to cry on. I trusted him and was amazed with how well he handled me. He encouraged me to allow Kevin back in and to go to counseling to deal with all the emotional devastation.

Chaz and I continued our sexual relationship. Initially, I considered Chaz an option for a potential relationship, but as time went on parts of his personality began to worry me. I started to believe some of the sociopath rumors I heard from women who dealt with him before me.

The most shocking rumor came from a man that knew Chaz. He said Chaz used to date his sister and her experience with him was damn near criminal. He said Chaz had some sick fetish with getting women pregnant and then aborting the baby. It was an empowerment thing. I started to notice some of those characteristics and I made Valentine's day 2006 the last day Chaz and I would spend together.

I let Chaz take me to dinner for the holiday. He and I had had sex earlier that week before I found out about his weird fetish. I was paranoid that he would try to open Pandora's box after dinner, so I was going to conveniently get sick before the bill came.

We went to a small restaurant in downtown Columbus. It was quiet and secluded. Many of the white collar workers would go there to have their business meetings and do wine tastings. I didn't see too many black folks in that place and looking at the menu I could tell why. Cucumber sandwiches and tuna tartare and shit. We like fancy things but comfort food is more enticing.

I just went with it and prayed the steak was seasoned well. Halfway through the meal, the waiter presented me with a card that had a purple heart above my name. I only knew one person who dotted the "i" in my name with a heart. I looked around the restaurant to see if I saw him, but the only other black person I saw was the pianist and a guy at the bar when we first walked in.

I opened the note to see if my suspicion was correct and it was. Derric was in town and wanted to see me. I was speechless. I was sure I had ruined the rest of his heart with the news of the abortion. I wrapped up dinner telling Chaz there was a family emergency and left in a hurry, catching a cab back to my car.

After going home to quickly change, I practiced what I was going to say to Derric in the mirror. I knew I loved him and didn't want to lose him, but something in me wanted to continue to work things out with Kevin. If I had a choice I wouldn't raise my son in a broken environment. But I didn't want to tell Derric that, I just wanted to enjoy the time we had together.

My visit with Derric was short and sweet. I could tell he was still very much in love, but I couldn't give him all of me. I struggled with holding Derric's heart hostage. I felt like I needed it in case I got hurt. I wasn't sure what Kevin and I were going to do, but I was still married and I would have rather worked out my marriage and run off with Derric's heart than to divorce Kevin with the possibility of breaking my son's heart.

I was conflicted and torn internally; the idea of a complete family kept me in bondage. I left Derric that night unsure of what the future would hold. I prayed hard that night for God to help me. I only knew one prayer by heart and I screamed it over and over again:

Lord give me the serenity to accept the things I cannot change, the courage to change the things I can, and the wisdom to know the difference!

Lord give me the serenity to accept the things I cannot change, the courage to change the things I can, and the wisdom to know the difference!

Lord give me the serenity to accept the things I cannot change, the courage to change the things I can, and the wisdom to know the difference!

March 15, 2006 was a memorable day. I took Ka'John to the barber shop and upon arrival, another kid was already sitting in the chair at the same time of our appointment. Of course it would be a day when I was already behind and in a rush to get out of there.

I sat next to the mother of the young client with my face turned up, discreetly shooting daggers at the barber for double booking us. The mother of the boy quickly acknowledged my frustrations and quietly said, "Isn't being booked and busy a blessing?"

I looked at her and wondered how she could turn this irritating situation into a church session, but out my mouth came an "Amen." I wasn't one to be outright with praise in public, so meeting someone who was seemingly young and full of glory looked strange to me. The lady introduced herself as Tisha and embraced me with a hug. This all happen so fast, I didn't have enough time to feel violated. I didn't normally pick up women in barbershops so this was new.

Tisha was vibrant and you could tell she had a healthy relationship with God. I almost envied the way she freely spoke about God and spewed off scriptures. She asked me about my kids and if I was married. I simply responded yes; I didn't feel the need to tell her my life story.

She shared the fact that she was 28 and had three kids ages 5, 9, and 12. Two girls and one boy. She then went on to say say she *had been* married, but her husband was murdered.

I remember gasping. She was so young, with three children, by herself, and to go through the tragedy of losing a husband and the kids losing a father... I didn't even want to imagine.

Immediately I felt a closeness to her that I didn't have before I knew that information. I felt sympathy and began to question how she was living so vividly under those circumstances. She belonged to a church not too far from where I lived and she invited me out. I wasn't sure if I was going to contact her, but we exchanged numbers and at least made the attempt.

Making friends as adults was not as natural as when we were in school. Although we seemed to have some sort of connection, I was pretty convinced that was the last time I would see her unless we bumped into each other at the shop.

Tisha's story about her husband got me thinking about my own marriage. God forbid anything happen to Kevin; I would die of heart break for Ka'John. Ironically enough, Kevin was coming around more and he would show up at my apartment a few times a week unannounced. He eventually told me he wanted to change his life around and wanted his family back. I had already filed the divorce papers; however, I still hadn't received a court date.

Even with being up against a divorce, Kevin offered to go to church with me. Unbeknownst to him, he won me over with that alone. God was becoming more prevalent in my life and it was important to me that we were on the same page with our faith. Kevin and I talked about moving back in together, but I stressed the fact that I wanted to start fresh. I didn't want him to move in with me; I wanted us to get a place that was ours.

As we searched for places, we maintained our own space and continued to live apart. I still didn't completely rid myself of other guys until I knew for sure what was going to happen with our marriage or divorce.

I hadn't talked to or responded to Derric since Valentine's day. He didn't live in Ohio anymore so at times it was an out of sight, out of mind kind of thing.

I wanted to break things off with Donte; he was getting way too serious about me and all I wanted to do was keep him in the friend zone. During Donte's eleventh hour, he reminded me of a wedding that I agreed to accompany him to. I thought this would be a good farewell date.

Donte and I had a blast. I wore flats that day so I didn't hover over him too much. The after party had an open bar and it was the first time I drank hard liquor. I blacked out after three shots of Hennessy and somehow I made it home. I woke up with my pajamas and my scarf on so I assumed I had been a responsible drunk. I didn't hear from Donte after that; I suppose he got the clue.

I hadn't talked to Chaz since I bailed on him during dinner. He didn't even check to see if I made it home that night so that transition came easy.

On April 1, 2006, Kevin and I moved into our first official apartment with both of our names on it. Kevin put in a lot of effort to help me forget his old ways. He sold his

"Hot Boy" truck, gave up the street life and got a legit job. He seemed like he wanted to become a true family man. He talked about having more kids and he shared with me a dream he had the night before. He said he dreamed that I was pregnant and had the baby 10 months from then. I did not entertain the thought. I wanted to focus on getting back on track to see if we would work out.

He seemed to have a whole new attitude and he made the effort to make amends with people who he previously didn't get along with. He and my mother even shared a moment together, which was almost synonymous to hell freezing over.

When we got settled into the apartment, it was just the three of us again. We spent a lot of time hanging out in Ka'John's room. He was becoming a big boy and we gifted him with a more mature style. He graduated from a crib to a fireman toddler bed. He had been obsessed with firemen ever since Kevin took him to his uncle's fire station.

To add our finishing touches to his big boy room, we all dipped our hands in paint and made hand marks on his wall for fun. Ka'John was a bit of a young rebel and dipped his whole leg in the paint and karate kicked the wall. Kevin and I looked at each other and smiled, knowing there were many more memorable moments like that one to come.

Kevin and I were down to one car since he got rid of his truck. On On April 3, 2006, my car overheated and we were stuck in the apartment. We called family and friends to help us get around. My friend, Nika, was the first to come to our rescue. I left with her to run errands and get some groceries in case we were stuck longer than expected. We were gone several hours because I got lost in trying to find Blue Moo ice cream, which was Kevin and Ka'John's favorite. I failed desperately at that attempt, which I would later regret. When we got back to the apartment, Kevin's sister was in my kitchen making tacos. She wasn't my favorite person and I felt annoyed with her manning my appliances.

After dinner, Kevin left with his sister to go to the store for what should have been a quick smoke run. As he was walking out of the door, I was sitting at the desk, holding Ka'John in my lap, his face was full of taco sauce and stripped down to only his diaper. I was fixed on my computer typing a letter to my dad, trying to figure out how to address him. Should I say, "Hey Dad, Heeeey there!, Hi Father, Greetings, Arthur?" I couldn't figure it out. As Kevin walked out the door, he said "Bye Baybuh, love you." I stayed facing the computer and waved him off. He was only going to the corner store; I didn't want to break my concentration.

Time seemed to get away from me. I didn't realize I was typing the letter for almost two hours and only had three paragraphs. Overthinking at its finest. I happened to glance at the clock and it was almost 10 pm. I was confused about why it was taking so long for Kevin to get back from the store.

Just as I was getting ready to call around, I heard a frantic knock at the door. It shook me so much, I damn near dropped the baby. I yelled from the top of the steps, asking who it was.

In a distressed voice, Kevin's sister answered. Without thinking I ran down the steps and opened the door. Her face told 1,000 stories, but all I wanted to know was what was happening. She had Kevin's phone in her hand

and was repeatedly saying, "Kevin passed out." The medics were called to the scene and they took him to the hospital. My first thought was he got ahold of some bad weed, but as I got in the back of the car, a gush of wind came over me. I checked the windows and all of them were up. An indescribable peace flowed over me.

Kevin died the next day. A brain aneurysm. I sat by the bed before they pulled the plugs and attempted to talk to God. I grew angry at him after for letting it happen. I didn't understand why He would allow such a cruel thing to happen to my family. All of my life I had done everything to prevent becoming a statistic and it seemed God was working against me. I immediately thought of Tisha and understood why meeting her was necessary. God was going to use her to carry me through this.

It didn't take me long to realize I was not in control. I had been attempting to create my own path my whole life when God already had one cleared out for me. I wasn't sure how this would work out for our good, but I reached back to my very first lesson and decided to find comfort in what I at least knew which was that God loves me and He would never leave me. So I fully expected Him to come down from the Heavens to help me raise my son.

After the funeral, Kevin's mother called me to tell me I had mail at her house. I didn't want to be in anyone's presence so I had her open the mail and just read it to me. Turns out, I had filed the wrong paperwork for the divorce and the courts threw it completely out. I suppose it didn't make much of a difference at that point.

I remembered Kevin's dream about me having a baby and with all the commotion in those two weeks, I didn't even notice I missed my period. I decided to take a pregnancy test only to be more devastated when the test came back positive.

I pleaded with God to take me, just end my life. I was now a widowed single mother of one and a half children. Every time I thought I was getting stronger in faith, something else happened to knock me back down. My mind began playing tricks on me and I started counting back the weeks since Kevin and I had sex. Something didn't add up.

Then my worst fear overtook me. Could I have been a duped by Chaz? Could he have purposely taken off those condoms and now I'm facing the consequences? How could I know for sure? How could I go through with this pregnancy knowing I'm carrying another man's baby? But how could I get rid of a baby that could possibly be a blessing from my husband that he left behind.

I was sick with conflict. In this very moment, I decided to challenge God to make this baby be Kevin's and forgive me for all my foolish ways. I was convinced He heard my prayer.

He Said

Chapter 10:
Dying Love

I was sick that Gloria had aborted my child. This was literally the worst news I had ever received to date. Not only that, but I also had to live with the fact that Sophia was pregnant with my child, which was the next-to-worst news to date.

As hypocritical as it might sound, I wanted Sophia to have an abortion. I _did not_ want to have a baby with her. I knew she was going to have this baby and there was nothing that I could do about it except try and pray the baby away. I felt like God owed me that favor. But in the end, I knew I would have to be the man my father wasn't and take care of this baby.

Sophia and I moved in together a few months after I had found out she was pregnant. It was one of the many things I grudgingly did in that relationship. All we did was fight and argue. She labeled me as a terrible boyfriend, but continued to stay. She would rather complain about how awful I was than leave. I stepped out on her regularly and was very cavalier about it. I hated my life and everything about it. I was supposed to be in California producing music and jet-setting. But instead I was being held hostage by a pregnant crazy chick. We came to resent each other but stayed together. Sophia made it clear that she and my son were a package deal. So I stayed. I couldn't let history repeat itself with my child. I cared more about stopping generational curses than my own well being.

On August 11, 2005 my son was born. I was in the delivery room with Sophia while she was giving birth. Watching my son's birth was striking, a moment I didn't think I would embrace. I stood there in shock looking at my newborn child as he took his first breath and made his first sound. Out of nowhere I busted out crying. The joy of seeing a life that I had helped create was indescribable. I didn't realize I was capable of feeling so overwhelmingly happy and immediately connected to a child I initially wanted to deny.

Outside of that moment, I was having an emotional breakdown internally. Even during the most exhilarating moment of my life where I should have been focused on the present, Gloria was never far from my thoughts. I couldn't help but think how that moment should have been shared with her and not another woman.

That first year was rough and many times I thought about taking my son and leaving. But who was I kidding? A young black man on the run with a half black baby, I could see the Amber Alert going crazy in every state.

I liked the idea of being a father, and surprisingly, I enjoyed my son. I had to contain my happiness around Sophia because she would sabotage anything that brought a smile to my face. She would find a way to use those things that made my heart soft to her advantage, knowing exactly how to manipulate me in order to get what she wanted. I started to pretend I didn't like certain things just so she wouldn't find a way to pick it apart. I spent a lot of time sharing my thoughts with my eight-month-old, because I trusted him with all my heart.

I was thankful for the military. My experiences gave me the outlet I needed to keep me from going crazy with my home life. The downside was not getting to see my family in Ohio as much as I liked, primarily my mom and grandma. We would talk on the phone often and many times my mom would talk me off the ledge when Sophia and I got into it. My mom never complained or grew weary of my emotional dependency. She knew she was the only other escape I had and made sure to support me in every way.

After awhile I stopped badgering my mom with bottomless frustrations about my baby's mother and I allowed alcohol be the problem solver. I spent tons of money on my newfound habit, leading to a downward spiral. I wasn't managing money properly. I was spending carelessly and I failed to take into consideration that I was now financially responsible for a whole other human. I was a new father and at the lowest point of my life emotionally, financially and mentally.

I would find myself feeling sad out of nowhere, even on my best days, which was far and few in between. Even then I still felt empty. There were days I didn't want to get out of the bed and didn't care what responsibilities I had. The idea of sleeping my day away became more encouraging than having to confront the day and be disappointed. My mood began to affect my performance in the Air Force and I was referred to a psychologist. I was diagnosed with depression and was facing discharge. I was relieved that I was diagnosed and could possibly get help with feeling better. I thought that might be half the battle.

I thought about Gloria every day. Even though we had not spoken in awhile, I missed her like crazy. I looked at my life and realized it was spinning out of control. In an effort to gain some sort of power back, I began to face things I was afraid to confront.

Valentine's Day was approaching, marking four years since the first time Gloria and I made love. I didn't care who she was with or what was going on, I had my mind made up I was going to see her. I wasn't sure what I was going to do or say, but I knew I was being led to be in her presence, even if it was just for a moment.

I wanted to give her yellow roses, which solidified our friendship, and one single red rose to remind her that she is the only woman I'd ever loved. I left Albuquerque with only a book bag, my cell phone and my wallet, and I caught the bus to Ohio without telling Sophia a thing.

When I arrived in Columbus on Valentine's day, I knew I had limited time to find Gloria and say what I needed to say. I called all of her old jobs attempting to track her location. I finally got ahold of her cousin Leslie who told me she would be at a specific restaurant at 7 p.m. I had exactly 8 hours to get a plan together. I knew she would be with her guy, so I had to be strategic.

I sat at the bar adjacent from the door and waited until she arrived. She walked in at 7:05 looking as beautiful as the first day I saw her. Walking behind her was her "date," some corny-lookin' nigga with a tight ass suit and pointy shoes, looking nothing like Kevin. I waited for them to be seated before I asked the wait staff to send her a note. I simply wrote: *Four years ago today, we shared a special day. I loved you then, I love you still, I love you now, and always will. Meet me at my mom's house at 10 p.m. -Derric 831.* I watched her face light up and then her smile quickly dissipated as her date dude looked her dead in her face as if she was not allowed to express happiness without him. I laughed to myself and left out the side door.

I fully anticipated Gloria's arrival and I got my old room dimmed and ready to pour my heart out to her. She arrived at 11 p.m. only to stay for less than an hour. Enough time for me to give her roses and have one last intimate moment before she told me she couldn't get over the idea of me having a child.

She also mentioned there was a possibility of she and Kevin making their marriage work. Kevin was technically her husband, but she was out with a nigga that wasn't him and was here with me. She said one thing, but her body said different. She had a way of stringing me along and making me feel like there was some hope. Before she left that night, I made it clear that I had never wanted a family with anyone but her. She brushed it off, kissed me on my forehead and left.

I didn't talk to or hear from Gloria after that. I guess I expected her to fall for my efforts of wearing my heart on my sleeve, but she wasn't moved. A few months later, I got news that Kevin died. Ironically enough, my first concern was how Gloria was doing. I never wanted her to feel any pain or heartache, even under the circumstances. I can't say that hearing about Kevin's death affected me one way or the other. I didn't know him personally. I just viewed him as someone Gloria loved that I obviously couldn't compete with. My concern had always been for Gloria's wellbeing and all I wanted to do was make sure she was okay. I cared for her deeply, even though, at times, I felt like the feelings weren't mutual.

My next thought after making sure Gloria was okay was that we could finally be together now that Kevin could no longer be in the picture. As much as I hoped for the moment Gloria would completely give herself to me, I teetered on the line of not wanting to be the fallback guy. I wanted to feel like the only one for Gloria. I wanted to be as special to her as she was to me. I knew I wasn't her first choice, but I was willing to settle for her to want me in the same way that she wanted Kevin. She was always my number one priority, but I began feeling like I was just an option for her when things didn't work out with Kevin.

I attempted to reach out to Gloria after I heard about Kevin's passing. Her previous phone numbers were disconnected and I received a Return to Sender on a letter I mailed to her. I knew I had to make another trip to Ohio to make sure she was mentally intact. Knowing what it was like to be impaired emotionally, I wanted to protect her from anything that would possibly cause her harm even if it was internal.

It took me several months, but I was able to save enough money to book a flight to Ohio. That was the motivation I needed to stop drinking and gather myself. I didn't tell Sophia I was leaving this time either. I just left hoping that she would think I broke up with her and move out while I was gone. Wishful thinking.

I liked to see the smile on my mom's face when I popped up on her. I didn't tell her I was going to be in Columbus, so I looked forward to the surprise factor. I hadn't seen my mom since my son was born and even then it was only for a few hours. I was happy I was finally able to have her all to myself without any interruptions from Sophia.

When I arrived, my mom was cooking my favorite pie, lemon meringue, almost as if she knew I was coming. She opened the door with her mixer in one hand and homemade filling in the other and greeted me with the biggest hug. The excitement only lasted a few moments until she realized I didn't bring her grandson. Then she playfully didn't want anything else to do with me. No one told me you become secondary to your parents once your own children are born.

She had an idea of why I was in town. My mom knew how I felt about Gloria, and while other people would consider me a fool, she admired my passion. My mom thought I was amazing for my diligent pursuit and reminded me I was the last of a dying breed. She never discouraged me from loving someone who was difficult to love. She only told me I was a stronger person for the way that I loved. I can remember her telling me when I was in highschool, *"It's easy to love someone when everything is good. It's when things aren't going as planned that true love either shines or fades away, and if it fades, then it was never love."* Despite every adversity Gloria and I went through, I still felt the same about her. I was in love with her.

I went by Gloria's old job at the mall to see if I could surprise her there. I was told she hadn't worked there in months and might be working at the Victoria's Secret down the hall. As I attempted to make my way down the mall, I saw Gloria walking with someone who looked like a coworker. To my surprise Gloria was very much pregnant.

I was thoroughly confused. Kevin had passed away approximately seven months before and she looked to be about six to seven months pregnant. I couldn't move. Kevin just couldn't bow out gracefully, could he? He had to mark his territory again?

This had to be Kevin's baby. She wouldn't dare let another nigga get her pregnant and KEEP it, not when she got rid of my child. I had so many questions, but I could feel the anger rising. So I walked in the opposite direction to leave the the mall and left Ohio drowning in my sorrow. I turned back to the only thing that could make me forget my problems. Tequila.

She Said

Chapter 11:
Miraged

On December 17, 2006, my second boy was born. Tisha was the only one in the hospital with me at the time of his birth. She had remained an essential part of my spiritual growth from the moment I called her after Kevin died through the birth of my second child. She hadn't left my side.

However, I wanted to be the first person, aside from the doctor, to look at this baby face to face. I was anxious to see what he looked like. I knew once I saw him I would be able to immediately tell if the baby was Kevin's.

He was born after five hours of laboring. When the doctor placed him in my arms, my heart dropped from disappointment, and although Tisha had never met Kevin, she could tell immediately. As I held his little body to my bare chest, I quietly cried out to God and asked why. Why did He choose to complicate my life with an illegitimate child? Why did He leave me here to fend for myself? Why did God hate me? These were all the questions that ran through my mind seconds after I gave birth.

I just sat there, attempting to figure out how I was going to explain to Kevin's family that this child was not his. Even allowing the words to manifest inside my head seemed wrong, so I decided to allow them to come to their own conclusion.

I called Chaz to let him know the baby was born and it was a good idea to come see him and get tested. I now knew he was Chaz's baby; I hadn't been with anyone else. But legally, in order for Chaz to eventually have rights, he had to "prove" the baby was his.

Any time a married woman loses a spouse mid-pregnancy, by law the deceased spouse is assumed to be the parent and placed on the birth certificate. I used that as my gateway to walk into denial. I convinced myself that the baby's brown skin came from my mother's side of the family and his nose hadn't come into its own yet. This baby could still be Kevin's. So I named him accordingly: Kase Dottson.

The day I was due to leave the hospital, I got a few surprise visitors. Kevin's mom and sister. They insisted on seeing the baby and I had no choice but to give them that right. As the nurse wheeled Kase in from the nursery, my heart sank from anxiousness. It seemed like he had gotten darker from the night before. I was praying they didn't notice the difference like I did.

When he got there, they both smiled with excitement. Kevin's mom held him first. She barely looked at his face; she just held him close to her heart and whispered something in his ear. I held my breath until someone broke the silence.

His sister finally said, "Lemme hold him now, mah." She grabbed him gently under his arms and rubbed her cheek against his. She couldn't stop smiling and told him they were going to be "roll dogs." I couldn't tell if it was all an act or if they truly believed this was Kevin's child. And because I technically didn't know for sure, I assured myself that he was a Dottson.

I only took a week off of work after I had Kase. I was working at Victoria's Secret part-time and I had no benefits or paid time so I couldn't afford to miss work. My mom kept the boys while I worked, and although she wasn't the most nurturing being to me, she was a way better grandma. So I took advantage of her maturing ways. As time went on, Kase began to look different than Ka'John significantly and in my heart I knew everyone else knew. No one said a word. No one treated him different. No one shamed me. I did enough of that for everyone, and the guilt and embarrassment were overwhelming.

I called Chaz every few months to attempt to meet up with him to get tested. I noticed he would conveniently be out of town every time I'd call and each time he claimed he would set up something once he was back in the state. I didn't realize he was giving me the runaround until I saw him at a restaurant with a woman and two kids when he was supposed to be out of the country on business. I didn't understand the avoidance. I made it clear it wasn't a child support thing, although I could have used the money. The more pressing issue was the truth. I needed to clear my conscience of any lies I'd convinced myself of and he was holding up that process. He knew Kase was his son and he expressed concerns about being in the system once he officially handed over his DNA. I gave up trying to talk him into not running. I began trying to find my kids a dad so I could dispel any ideas of me being less than whole.

Although I was growing spiritually, I would still waver. My faith was not where it needed to be, but God was patient with me. Tisha introduced me to her church home and from the moment I walked in, I felt like that was the place to be.

The pastor spoke clearly, so much so he almost painted pictures with his words. He was a teacher atop of everything and that's exactly what I needed. I joined the church my first time visiting. I was searching for answers and needed to understand how I was in such a fucked up situation when I did everything right.

I caught myself thinking about Derric more. Every day I would replay our moments together in my head. I only allowed myself to wander away briefly because I was sure he was somewhere with his Puerto Rican princess and their cute biracial baby living the good life.

When I stumbled across a picture of his little family on his MySpace page, I felt sick immediately. He was good to me and I just handed him over to some bootleg J.Lo who was probably calling him Papi and baking sopapillas every night.

I needed to hurry up and become somebody's wife again.

Less than a year after Kevin's passing, I racked up two failed relationships and one engagement.

I should have known the engagement wasn't going to work; I wasn't "in love" with the guy. Hell, I wasn't even "in like" with him. He was just a safe option.

His name was Kerry Cole. He was a manager at Boston Market and didn't even own a cell phone. He was the complete opposite of Kevin. He wore his hair slicked back and his pants on his waist. His nails were always clean. Fortunately for him, his smile made him more attractive than what he was.

Kerry had initially approached me in the library. I was intrigued simply because of his mannerisms. He was 30 and I was barely 22, so oftentimes he wouldn't be able to relate to my late teen lifestyle. One thing that I lucked up on was him not having any children, which was rare for someone his age. I was relieved because I didn't have to worry about any crazy baby mothers lurking around. The guy I dated before him had a crazy ex-wife that busted out my windows in my minivan and wrote obscenities on my windows with lipstick. I didnt need those problems and as far as I knew, Kerry didn't have any recent exs.

As I got to know Kerry, everything he ever said he would do, he did. I found comfort and security in that. He had a weirdness about him that couldn't be explained. I thought it was from some sort of abuse because he would frequently talk about how hard his dad was on him and made mention to never being that way with his future kids. He also had been hurt by someone in the church so he was skeptical about attending traditional service.

We didn't have sex because both of us wanted to wait until marriage. We had been through a lot individually and mutually agreed it would complicate things. I thought about it often though. It seemed more intriguing because it was unattainable.

As I began to understand the difference between sex and love, I realized no one made love to me like Derric and everything else was an intimate fuck at best. I was nervous to wait. Kerry, I truly wanted to see what I was up against. I thought about him popping it out and it not extending longer than his testicles. He seemed like he had a small penis. He walked way too fast, indicating maybe there wasn't much to work with.

I happened to accidentally see what he was working with when I walked in on him pleasuring himself to gay porn. He didn't realize I walked in at first and I got a glimpse of him aggressively pounding his safely wrapped, approximately 5 inch long, 3 inch girth penis with a grapefruit. His slicked back hair was wildly flapping forward as he took each stroke and his face nearly froze as I caught him in mid-orgasm.

When he realized he had company, he jumped up and quickly pulled his pants back over his belly button. He was embarrassed and couldn't stop apologizing. I felt like I had been cheated on. I certainly know what that feels like and it was comparable to that. He later told me he had a porn addiction and wanted to get help.

When he asked me to marry him months after the Porn-Gate incident, I hesitantly said yes, although I knew I was going to take that back after the excitement wore off. He went through too much trouble for me to shut it all down at that moment. I knew I didn't want to marry Kerry because I couldn't live with his sexual issues and his anal retentive personality.

I broke it off with Kerry in the spring of 2008. I was broken down by all the self-inflicted emotional bullshit. I finally decided to stop putting myself out there and spend time getting to know me as a person. I had been so wrapped up in finding a replacement for my replacement, that I didn't know what I liked anymore.

I spent a lot of time in my new church learning who God was. At one point I was so on fire for the Lord, I'd cast down evil spirits on guys who approached me in the wrong way because surely the enemy sent them to distract me. I became a born again virgin and was so churchy, only people who spoke Bible could talk to me. As time went on, I found a balance. I began engaging with other young adults at the church I attended and realized God is not looking for spiritual perfection, only spiritual progression.

There were times when I felt so lonely from lack of intimacy, I would crawl up in a ball and cry until I got a headache. The kids would comfort me by kissing me on the cheek and forehead and I would be temporarily content with their efforts. When I looked at the both of them I felt an overwhelming feeling of sadness. What have I done? What kind of life have I created for them? As they both sat there unaware of their future struggles with becoming men without a father, I determined I would continue to fight. I took the control back from God and decided I had a better plan.

I started going out more often. If I wanted to get a husband, I needed to be seen. I hung out at the local clubs and wore the sexiest outfits. I was usually the main attraction and I wouldn't have had it any other way. I only had one rule: I wouldn't dance with people that I didn't know. I knew a lot of people so I hardly had an issue, but I put this rule in place after being groped and touched so many times by strangers, it felt too much like childhood.

I was out one night with a few my cousins, when a group of guys approached us. The group I was with seemed to know the guys so they became friends of mine. I made an exception to the stranger danger rule this one time since there were extenuating circumstances. The smallest guy came up from behind me and started grinding my butt. I quickly turned around to check him out to see if he was grinding material and I wasn't too impressed.

He was a few inches taller than me, definitely weighed less than me and he looked like he was an African. I steered away from African men. They seemed too aggressive. I politely shimmied away and slowly turned back around only to see him grinding the air. He didn't notice my cha cha slide away; he was way too into it.

Later we all went to the Waffle House and in comes the guy group from the club, the African-looking dude was with them and I instantly shook my head. I knew he was going to try and shoot his shot.

Waffle House was well lit so I got a better look at him in the light. He didn't look too bad, but I was waiting for him to open his mouth; that would determine if he was decent or not. When he saw me, he came over and gave me a hug. I took a step back and got nearly blinded by his pearly whites. He had a beautiful set of teeth and I allowed myself to be entertained by whatever was going to come out of his mouth.

We all parted ways that night and I couldn't help but be disappointed. I didn't see any real potential. All the guys who liked me were either drug dealers or missing a chromosome.

I spent months hanging out trying to get chosen and I was close to giving in until I received a special visit from Derric. He had completed his duties in the military and had come back home to visit. I had so many questions and I was surprised one of his first stops was to see me. I hadn't seen him since Valentine's Day of 2006. So much had happened since then. I felt like this was God's way of taking back the wheel. This had to be it. Derric and I had history. He always came back no matter what. I had been too selfish to see that he was what I needed. I embraced him and began to cry. I felt almost as if I was being rescued.

He told me he never stopped loving me regardless of the things that happened between us and that he thought about me every moment of every day. As we stood at my doorway, I could hear screams coming from his car. I looked at him, he looked at me, I looked at the car, then back at him, and he softly said, "Oh, that's Pedro."

Pedro? His son with the Puerto Rican princess. My heart dropped. I knew he had a child, but it didn't seem real until right then. I was crushed. I never had to share him with anyone. Now I had to be a stepmom to a kid that should have been mine, hypothetically speaking. Derric asked if we could spend some time together and I obliged. He dropped Pedro off with his mom and came back to stay with me.

We spent an entire week together, barely leaving each other's side. We talked about the possibilities of living together in a different state and we shared many intimate moments. I missed his touch. I knew he loved me by the way he looked at me. He would gaze at me as if I were the only woman in the world and then smile as if I was a gift from God. He made me feel beautiful.

I was not going sabotage this love ever again. We briefly talked about the elephant in the room which was Kase. I didn't admit that Kase was Chaz's son to Derric. He already believed he was Kevin's child and it was easier that way. I couldn't very well tell him I got pregnant by someone else, especially when I chose not to keep his child.

He wasn't too fond of the idea that I had had another child, and I knew once he laid eyes on him, he would call bullshit. I knew there was no way to avoid that moment, but I certainly prolonged it as long as possible.

The day Derric had to leave, we spent less time together than usual. He was going back and forth trying to pack and get his son prepared for their departure. He left to get some items from his mom's, but he assured me he would return a few hours before he was scheduled to leave so we could have some more time.

As I was waiting on him to return, I got a phone call from an unknown number. I answered the call only to hear an unrecognizable female voice on the other end. She asked me if this was Gloria and I gave her a strong yes. I could tell she was calling on some bullshit because she was talking low and she called from a private number.

She proceeded to tell me her name was Sophia and she was Derric's girlfriend. I played it cool because I wanted to hear everything she had to say. Derric had always been honest with me so I had no reason to believe he did anything wrong. She told me that she was in Columbus and that she knew Derric had been at my house. Sophia proceeded to tell me he had been going back and forth between her house and mine and having sex with the both of us in this last week. She said she had followed him a few times and she knew where I live.

I began getting angry. I still played it cool with Sophia because she didn't need to see me sweat. But I couldn't wait to get off the phone to confront Derric. It's one thing to have a whole girlfriend, but to bounce dick back and forth is just reckless. As I started to get off of the phone because I had heard enough, she dropped one last bomb on me. "Oh, by the way, I'm three months pregnant with our second child."

Chills ran through my body and my eyes immediately started to tear up. I guess karma is a bitch. I congratulated her and hung up the phone. I tried to dial Derric's number, but my hands wouldn't stop shaking. I finally got a steady hand and aggressively dialed his phone. When he picked up, I didn't give him a chance to say anything.

I told him I knew about Sophia and the long distance threesome. I told him how horrible he was for putting me in a compromising situation and warned him to never call my phone, stop by my house or reach out to me again. I hung up and cursed God for allowing me to believe he was any different than any other man in my life.

He Said

Chapter 11:
Miraged

I had started a family with the wrong person and all I was doing was wasting my time and hers. I always knew I didn't want to be in that situation with Sophia, but I also thought my idea of the right person would come much easier than I experienced. I suffered through being rejected, looked over, dumped and much more just to end up still living a life I never wanted. After all of the bullshit I endured from Gloria, I still was very much in love with her. Maybe my mom was wrong. Maybe I was a fool. Whatever anyone wanted to call it, no matter what Gloria did, she still had my heart. I felt like I was in bondage in life and in love.

Sophia was still hanging around. She had threatened to leave with Pedro on several occasions and one time actually packed their bags and left. I didn't chase after her for my son because I was numb to the threats. She attempted to control me through my son and I was over it. She tried to convince me I was a deadbeat father for the way I treated her, for my lack of love for her and the way I refused to let her in.

I believed some of those things and began to think I didn't deserve to be a father to Pedro if I couldn't love his mother. I wanted my son to have everything I never had and I didn't think I was capable of giving him those things. As much as I loved Pedro, if I could do things differently, he would never have existed. He had become another source of so much unnecessary pain that I was willing to let him go just to experience peace again.

I had been dehumanized by Sophia and I don't know how I allowed it to get that far. I remember when I was younger being so rough around the edges that I wouldn't allow much to get to me, but she successfully got in my head and made me think I was less than a man.

When she left, it was only for 22 hours. She called saying she thought something was wrong with Pedro and she was rushing him to the hospital. I immediately jumped into parental mode. Regretting all all the resentful thoughts

I had about him being born, I was scared and I didn't want anything to happen to my son regardless of how I felt about his mother. When I arrived at the hospital, the doctor was preparing them for discharge. Pedro had pink eye. Sophia claimed she thought he was going blind.

I began to have anxiety about the idea of something happening to my son. I didn't trust Sophia and I put up with more of her foolishness just to ensure Pedro was safe. I often thought about Gloria's new baby. At this point it had to be at least a year old.

I wondered who the baby looked like. Was it a boy or girl? Who was helping her raise the baby? I never desired to be a stepfather and this was no exception. As much as I loved Gloria, I didn't know if I could ever look at her children and not be hurt, or for that matter, not see our child. I know our child had to be a girl. My mom always said girls are made out of love.

Sophia started going to a local church in Albuquerque. At first I thought it was a great idea. Maybe someone could pray some of that hell up out of her. But after several months of her consistently attending, I noticed

199

a change in her attitude that was potentially worse than the issues she had prior to getting saved. She became "holier than thou" and began pointing out my sinful ways. She ultimately made me feel like God loved her more than me because she went to church every week. She began to put the pressure on me to marry her because we were "living in sin." But I felt like marriage was not going to undo the sin so why would we need to go that far?

The thought of marrying Sophia made me physically sick. I didn't understand how we got to this point where she would consider me husband material or think she was the wife of my dreams. The only time I ever thought about marriage was with Gloria and that's as far as I ever wanted it to go. I didn't want Sophia to get the wrong idea and actually think I loved her. I played house for my son. I had sex with her for my own physical needs. And I tolerated her because of lack of options.

I put that option as far back in my mind as possible. Sophia started forcing me to go to church with her saying she needed help with Pedro, but in reality it was a set up. Every week someone different would come up to us saying what a lovely family we have and ask how long we have been married. She was always quick to say it hasn't happened yet and that she was waiting for that moment. All I could think of was that she would be waiting until her twat hairs turn grey.

She eventually got the pastor to corner me. He was a small white man with a deep receding hairline and slight lisp. He called me into his office one day after service to talk "kingdom business." I already didn't trust him. Any man who keeps his office a mess in the "house of the Lord" is suspicious. I've always heard that cleanliness is next to Godliness.

He ran off all kind of scriptures about what it means to be head of household, what a "real man" does and how I should have been seeking to be the best man of God I could be. This man didn't know me from Adam, but he claimed God told him to relay a message. I called bullshit. God knows how to get in touch with me directly. I walked out of his office with my mind made up. I was breaking up with Sophia. I didn't want anyone forcing my hand anymore.

When I got back to the apartment, I started packing her shit. I wanted her to know I wasn't playing and I was done with the control she had over me regarding our son. When she got home, she was shocked. She had never lost power like this and had very few godly words to say. She claimed she didn't have anywhere to go and I suggested she go to the same 55 places she was going to go when she threatened to take my son all those times. When she became physical, I pushed her out the front door and locked her out, keeping my son right by my side. I made sure to call the police first so she couldn't lie and say I abused her. She went to jail that night for domestic violence.

I was at an advantage with our son because of her poor choices. After Sophia settled all the criminal issues, she left Albuquerque. Of all places to go, she settled in Ohio. My mom took her in until she got on her feet and got a job. Per court recommendation, she was to have Pedro one weekend a month.

I was officially discharged from the military in 2008. My depression got worse before it got better and my duties became overwhelming. I needed to get out of Albuquerque. I'd racked up just as many bad memories there as I did in Ohio. I considered moving to South Carolina. I'd heard good things and one of my military buddies gave me a referral for a job that made pretty good money. I was ready to make a change.

While I was in limbo, I would travel to Ohio to take Pedro to see Sophia. The only reason I stuck my neck out is because she was in Columbus and there was a good chance I would see Gloria. I went a week before Easter as I thought it would be a good time to spend with family. My main priority was to find Gloria and get the answers my soul desired. The last time I saw her she was very much pregnant and I couldn't bring myself to approach her. But I needed to clarify some things. I don't know if I was seeking closure or another heartache.

It took me nearly two days to get to Ohio, stopping a total of nine times because of the limited amount of urine a 2-year-old's bladder can hold. The whole time I was doing my best skip tracing to find out where Gloria lived. I got a tip from a reliable source and decided to go straight there once I reached the city. I pulled up to the address and my heart sank. All the bad memories and feelings started to rush back and I got anxious about getting out of the car. I didn't know what to expect and I wasn't sure why I kept setting myself up to get disappointed, but the love I had for her overshadowed any doubt or fear of rejection.

I knocked on the door and at that very moment I considered walking away. I had my son in the car and if another naked nigga came to the door trying to fight, I didn't want my son being there. As I started to step back, Gloria came to the door and looked at me as if she had seen a ghost. I couldn't tell right away if she was happy to see me or if she was disgruntled. She embraced me right away and everything in me stood still. She still gave me that same feeling. The way she touched me was unmatched.

We caught up on the porch for almost 15 minutes until I realized Pedro was in the car. I could tell she wasn't ready to face those realities, so I quickly made my exit. I told her I would drop him off and would come back to hang out with her if she was available. We had a lot to catch up with and I was eager to get back. As I pulled away, I imagined her house being our home and Pedro being our son, and me dropping him off at his grandma's for the weekend so we could get away. I wanted that to be our reality.

As I pulled up to Sophia's apartment, I got an eerie feeling. That was the moment I wished that little girl from *Bewitched* was real. I'd wiggle the hell out of her nose to be someone else at the time. Sophia greeted me at the door, she was practically naked with just a towel around her head and one around her chest. I was irritated that she didn't take care of her hygienic needs prior to our arrival. I walked straight past her into the empty one bedroom apartment and stood close the front door. There was nowhere to sit and I was concerned about leaving my son in such a resourceless place, but getting back to Gloria overthrew my concern for their comfort.

From where I was standing I could see the one room she did have at least had a bed and a crib. I laid Pedro down in the crib and proceeded to head out. Sophia began to cry and asked if we could talk. I didn't think there was much for us to talk about, but I had never seen her cry so I was interested to see what she was going to say.

She started off apologizing for everything she ever did. She told me I was an amazing father and complimented my mom for her singlehanded job. I was shocked. The nicest thing she had ever said to me until that point was,

"Your pasta wasn't hard this time." And that was before Pedro was born.

She gave me a hug that seemed more intimate than a church hug and began taking off my belt. I had a decision to make. While I was thinking, she bought me some time and began *kneeling at the altar*. I couldn't help but wonder if she considered what she was doing was a sin. I let it happen for a while until I couldn't stay hard. It felt wrong and I didn't want her to get the wrong idea.

I pulled up my pants and left in a hurry. I didn't bother staying to gather myself or wash off. I didn't want it turning into anything else. I got about five blocks away before I realized I must have dropped my phone. I did an immediate U-turn and headed back to Sophia's place.

As I approached her door, I knocked first. I didn't want to get that familiar with her by walking in. I knocked for what seemed like five minutes before I decided to try the knob. The door was unlocked so I walked in calling out her name. The apartment seemed empty and even Pedro was not in his crib. I thought it was strange that she would leave so quickly after I left, but as I headed out, I heard a small voice in the closet of her room and decided to open it.

There she was, sitting cross-legged with her hand over my son's mouth and my open phone in her other hand. I snatched my phone and my son and headed back toward the door.

I dropped Pedro off with my mom. She always delighted in seeing her only grandson and was willing to keep him as long as necessary. I told her to have Sophia see Pedro at her house so she could monitor her. She seemed to take pride in having that responsibility. I trusted my mom to make sure everything went smoothly. I was anxious to get back to Gloria.

Gloria and I spent a lot of time together during that week. I got most of my questions answered and while I can't say I felt better about everything, I can say after everything was said and done, I still wanted her to be part of my life. She poured her heart out to me and things seemed different this time. There was no one for me to play second fiddle to and she seemed to feel the same way that I've always felt. And that's all I'd ever wanted.

When the week ended, I had second thoughts about going back to South Carolina. I wanted Gloria and me to start a life. I wanted to her out of Ohio and push the restart button. I was determined to figure out how to make that happen.

As I was gathering Pedro's and my things to head back to Albuquerque, Gloria called. Just seeing her name come across my phone gave me a good feeling. I answered and knew immediately something was wrong. She was yelling and crying and cussing at me, which she had never done before. She said she knew about Sophia and what happened with us and she didn't want anything to do with me.

I was hot. I'd put up with all kinds of shit in the previous nine years and I get a little head and she is done with me? I didn't get a word in edgewise before she hung up and blocked my calls. I called Sophia and asked her what she did and her response was, "Nothing, let God's will be done."

I left Columbus with completely no hope that I'd ever speak to Gloria again. Maybe this was God's will.

She said

Chapter 12:
I Do

After all the smoke cleared, I finally understood that God needed me all to Himself. I didn't understand why He allowed certain things, but I knew my trials would eventually work out for my good. My relationship with Him was fragile and I needed to do my part to figure out how to repair it. I was determined to surrender. I was tired of failing at everything. I lost my husband, my boyfriend, my home, my job, and then my car all in a matter of two years. My head was so far in the clouds I hadn't even done my due diligence as a mother. The times when I thought I was pulling things together for my children to have a better life was time spent away from them focusing on the wrong things. I spent the following months in prayer, fasting and abstinence.

I decided to go to church with one of my friends from school. She had been inviting me for a few months and I always made excuses why I couldn't go. I was happy with my church and I didn't see a need to venture off to other churches. Besides, I heard they did strange things there and I wasn't spiritually advanced enough to not get somewhat pulled in by the foolishness.

On this particular Sunday, there was a guest pastor from TV that was going to be speaking at her church and I thought it would be cool to see someone from TV. When we got in the church, all the doors and windows were open. Most of the seats were full and it felt like we were having service right in the middle of hell because there was absolutely no air circulating. I didn't want to sit down because it was shoulder to shoulder and black folks give off too much heat. I was already sweating from standing in the doorway.

The guest pastor told everyone who was already sitting to raise their hand if there was a seat next to them so everyone could sit down. I considered leaving, but I didn't drive there. When we got our seats, the pastor was in the midst of "putting the Holy Ghost" inside of people by putting his mouth up against the microphone and humming. The humming could be felt in the pews as it hit the speakers and vibrated against the floor.

Shortly after, people started jumping and yelling. Some even performing acrobatic moves. I sat and looked around at the strange worship and held onto Kase as if to not get sucked in by this seemingly dangerous Holy Ghost. Just when I thought the excitement was over, the guest pastor decided to start throwing gallons of water in the audience. This was their form of cleansing or baptizing everyone at once. I also was not in agreeance with this tradition; I just got my hair straightened out the day before and didn't see any sense in wasting good water. I stepped outside until everyone else got baptized.

I knew there was some things that God himself may not have agreed with in this church, but I stayed and silently talked to God. As I was sitting there listening to the pastor scream at the top of his lungs about the magical number 40, he did an altar call for everyone to sow forty dollars and be blessed by God.

Silently to God, I called bullshit, but I also told God that He knew that was all the money I had left in this entire world, and me putting forty dollars in that bucket wasn't a sign of me believing what the pastor was saying, but it was walk of faith. It was a sacrifice that I would make for all the times I hadn't trusted Him in the past. It was a covenant that I would put my ways down and pick His up. And right then, I shook hands with God and I gave my last forty dollars to the screaming, water-throwing, vibrating pastor. I left feeling like God was happy with me.

The weeks following the ridiculous church service, God made good on our handshake. I was offered a position making more money than I ever made with a sign on bonus. The bonus was enough for a down payment on a new car and a much needed vacation. Life was looking up for once and I was really rocking this independent woman thing. My kids were taken care of; I had a nice home, a new car and a job that would allow me the flexibility I needed as a single parent.

At times, I still got lonely. It was depressing going to bed alone every night only to wake up in a wet spot from both the boys sneaking in my bed and having a piss party in their sleep. I prayed God would send me someone who could help balance out my life. Even though I acknowledged God as being the head of my life, I was afraid to allow anyone else in because it seemed to me that's when things started going bad. I kept praying and asking God to prepare me for my future husband.

Going to the barbershop became a source of anxiety for me since that's where all the creeps hung out. It was another single mom chore I had to endure. On this particular day, I let Ka'John ride his bike to the barber shop and I pushed Kase in the stroller behind him. By the time we got to the barbershop, I was dehydrated and out of breath. I took a seat in the cool air and as I was sitting down, in walks the African-looking guy from the club a while back.

He had the most refreshing unopened drink, glistening with water crystals. Out of a desperate attempt to not die, I asked if I could have his drink. Without hesitation, he smiled and said, "Sure."

I drank it all in one gulp and then said, "Heeeey, how have you been? Thanks for saving my life, by the way." I didn't even know his name, but I was thankful he wasn't an asshole like I had been to him. I left the barbershop a little more flirty than I normally would be if he hadn't done me a favor. I figured I'd throw him a bone.

That next day, I received an inbox message on Facebook from the nice African. His name came up as Mark, which I thought was odd for his culture. He asked me out on a date and I felt obligated to say yes. We exchanged numbers and he set up a movie date. I began to chicken out because I could have sworn I saw him limping and what if he had a wooden leg? I wouldn't have been able to deal with that. So I called him and told him I had babysitting issues and I wouldn't be able to make it.

He knew the way to my heart because instead of bowing out, he offered to bring me food. I couldn't resist a free meal. I agreed to allow him to bring me food. This would be my opportunity to check out his leg and see if it was real.

As he pulled up, I was peeking through my blinds and watching him walk to the door. He had basketball shorts on which confirmed he had two authentic legs. I let him in and we had an unofficial first date right in my kitchen. We talked for hours and I got to know more about Mark. As it turns out, he wasn't African at all, just regular black. He was also a father of two, which was shocking because he looked like he had never had sex a day in his life. He started to grow on me and I after a while I began to think this was who God was preparing me for.

Mark proposed after we dated for six months and I said yes. Everything just fell into place easily and I was sure this was it. I couldn't say I had that same feeling with Mark that I had with Derric, but Mark was another safe option and he seemed to care about me as a total package. I thought if God allowed this to happen, this must be His will. Mark fit right into the missing puzzle piece and he even fit in well at my church. People loved us as a couple and supported our endeavors. That gave me a sense of acceptance. Although I had by then realized I was born to stand out, it still felt good to belong.

We seemed to find favor wherever we went. We got an offer from a reality TV show to film our wedding. We both decided that we couldn't let that opportunity slip away. Things were happening so fast; it seemed like a blessing from God.

Before Mark and I got married, we found a house and moved in together. In the spirit of breaking the house in, we found ourselves being intimate long before the wedding day. I had to sample the milk before buying the cow and I can't say that I was disappointed.

Two months before the wedding, I found out we were expecting. I didn't know how to feel about this unexpected surprise, but we were getting married anyway so I considered it a blessing. I didn't tell any of my family or friends; I wanted to wait until after the wedding to make it seem like we were in the proper order.

We got married on April 24, 2010. The wedding day was surprisingly beautiful. Everything came together and we didn't have any major problems.

The film crew from the reality show was with us the whole week up and through the wedding day. There was some genuineness taken from the wedding day with filming happening at the same time. Entertainment replaced some authenticity. Overall the experience was unique.

The wedding aired that September 2010 and we quickly became local celebrities. Our social media became inflated and we could really now use the term: "Google me." I had people in my inbox claiming me as their cousins from my mom's side and babysitters that used to watch me when I was a toddler.

The attention was intoxicating. I got caught up thinking I was more than I was. This was the very validation I needed to forget about my surrender to God and do what looked good. The dangerous thing about going outside of God's will to get what I wanted was I had to stay outside of His will to keep it.

I gave birth to my third son, Mason, on November 15, 2010. He was cuter than I imagined and although the thought of having another boy disturbed me throughout my whole pregnancy, I couldn't help but love him when I held him in my arms. He smiled at me when I sang to him as if he knew the melody by heart. He seemed to find comfort in my voice. I began to realize that of all the joys of becoming a woman, motherhood had to be the greatest.

I received tons of emails over the following year from people who saw me on TV, wanting to work with me or congratulate me on the new baby, but the email that would ultimately change my course came from Derric.

He didn't initially mention seeing me on TV he expressed more concern about my well-being and told me his sister was going to be graduating soon and that he would be in town for the ceremony. I was afraid he contacted me by happenstance and didn't know I was married or had another child. I certainly didn't want to be the bearer of bad news.

As we got deeper into the conversation, he admittedly told me he'd married Sophia, coincidently two months after Mark and I got married. The feeling of betrayal rushed over my body once again and it took me back to that moment in 2008 when I was bombarded with the news about Derric's second baby. I reluctantly responded that I was happy for him and his family. In an effort to conceal the fact that I was affected by that news, I asked about his kids. He quickly responded in capital letters: "KIDS?" I was confused by his response.

Derric asked me to call him and left his number in my email. I wasn't sure if I was ready to talk to him without getting emotional. Besides, I had been married for only a year. With a new baby and a family, I didn't need any distractions. We had had our chance and it was blown.

I went back to the email every day for a week before I decided to call him. I convinced myself he just wanted to catch up and we could be the best of friends within our circumstances. As I began to dial his number, my hands started to shake like they did when I frantically called his phone after his then girlfriend/baby mom had called me and dropped a bomb on me. When he answered, his voice was gentle and familiar. I quickly forgot about any issues we had had between us. I could feel the sincerity in his voice and I missed that.

He wanted to get right to clearing things up. He asked me why I put an "S" on kid when I knew he only had one. I told him I knew about his second child because the day I told him to never call me again I'd talked to Sophia and she told me everything. She'd straight out told me she was expecting another child and for me, that was the deal breaker.

Derric grew seemingly upset and began getting loud. He said that was a lie and he would never have another child with her or anyone else as long as he lived. Which didn't make a lot of sense to me seeing as he married her.

He told me that he hadn't wanted to marry her, but that she had given him an ultimatum. He would either have to marry her or she would move away with their son and he would never see him again.

This is how we know men are from Mars because if a man tried to keep a woman from seeing their child, most of us would shut the whole globe down before letting that happen. Unfortunately some men don't have that same passion and get bamboozled into thinking they are less than a rightful parent.

As we continued to exchange more information, I found out Sophia manipulated that whole situation. I didn't know how to feel. I was upset for not asking more questions and making decisions in such an emotional state. Had I not answered that phone call that day, the outcome would have been much different. I wouldn't have entertained Mark; I wouldn't have someone else's child. And I would have been saying, "I do," to someone who had always loved me, in spite of me.

He said

Chapter 12:
I do

      After Gloria told me she never wanted to speak to me again, I really didn't know what to do. I was offered a job in Charleston, SC, so I took it and moved there alone. I had moved there with the intention of trying to start my life over. I was getting paid more money than I had ever gotten paid in my life and I had benefits with a 401(k). In other words, this was my first real adult job. I was doing real important work, which was good because it made me focus on something other than my problems with Gloria. However, my nights were incredibly lonely and I found it hard to sleep.

      After about a month, Sophia came down to visit and basically demanded that we be together for our son. I figured Gloria would never speak to me again and she was the real reason I never let anyone else in, so I decided to settle. We were back together for only three weeks before she began putting the pressure on about marriage. After several ultimatums, bullying from her family members and fear of losing my son, I was semi-convinced it was the right thing to do. I asked her to marry me by writing it out on a toaster strudel.

As soon as we were engaged, her attitude turned sour again. She felt comfortable and entitled, beginning to control all that she could. I knew I was making a mistake, but everything up until this point was wrong anyway and I didn't have the strength or resources to change anything.

By this point, I was just going through the motions. I didn't help with the wedding plans at all. I didn't even give her an engagement ring; Sophia bought the wedding rings.

On June 26, 2010, I married her, something I said I would never do. I couldn't believe this was my life. The woman I loved hated me and I was stuck with a woman I didn't care for at all.

I didn't tell anyone in my family I was getting married until after it was over. I was in denial that I allowed this to happen and didn't want anyone I cared for to mistakenly believe this was what I truly wanted. The only people who showed up to our wedding were her friends and their husbands.

I avoided taking pictures; I didn't want any evidence of that day. There was a small reception after the "ceremony" and at that time I felt myself fall into a deeper depression. It was like I had no control over what was transpiring. I felt like I was just watching all these things materialize and I couldn't do anything about it.

At no point after we got married was I happy. There were days that were more tolerable than others, but ultimately I was just walking through it. There wasn't a day that went by that I didn't think about Gloria.

I began to journal again like when I was in the military. I wrote Gloria letters in my journal often. I apologized to her for not being Kevin, not being everything she wanted or needed and not being there to stop her from aborting our child. I apologized most of all for listening to her when she said to never speak to her again. I should have fought back. I would rather have fought with Gloria every day than to be with anyone else.

She had been so upset about me getting head from Sophia, but she hadn't realized there were no emotions attached with that. I'd never imagined Sophia would tell another woman she put her mouth on my junk. She must have been pretty desperate to put herself out there like that. I should have been honest with Gloria about what happened and maybe she would have understood. I had known Sophia was up to no good when I caught her with my phone.

Sophia would ask me about Gloria often. I didn't entertain her curiosity. I found pictures of Gloria on our computer that Sophia saved from my phone and the internet. I wasn't clear on why she wanted them. Her scheming ways were usually the source of our arguments. I would delete them every chance I got so she wouldn't have a chance of doing anything stupid.

To make matters worse, Gloria became a reality TV personality. My world was crushed again when I saw her wedding debut on national television. I was convinced Gloria was trying to kill me. Who was this random nigga?

Why was this being televised? And why was this giving Sophia so much life?

She would sit in front of the TV after a long day and watch the episodes from the DVR that she had previously recorded. She would sit there with a bag of popcorn and relish in that fact that Gloria was off the market looking happy with her soon-to-be husband. I'm assuming she thought that with Gloria out the way, I would give her that reserved love.

She was wrong. I would have rather died with it than give it away to someone who didn't deserve it.

I felt compelled to contact Gloria. I needed answers. Was this the real reason she blew me off? Was I really in competition with this goofy-looking nigga? I became furious. This was the fuel I needed to say all the things I had always been afraid to say. I didn't feel like I had anything to lose.

It took me months to get in contact with Gloria. I imagined with her newfound celebrity, my communication efforts had gotten lost in translation. I finally decided to use one of her old emails I had saved under her name and with that I got a response.

I made up some bullshit reason for reaching out in hopes she would receive me so I could eventually say what I needed to say. The first thing I *wanted* to say was, "WHAT THE FUCK," but I kept a cool head so we could build back a rapport. I was concerned about telling her that I married Sophia, but all that shit canceled out because she had had the nerve to marry someone who wasn't me.

I eventually told her about my marriage, but didn't press her for the information that I already knew. I wanted her to tell me. I wanted to hear the words come from her mouth that she had passed on me again.

We talked online for several weeks before I decided to give Gloria my work number. Sophia checked the itemized bill for any suspicious numbers and call times, so I felt it was safe for everyone to give Gloria an alternate number. There were just some things I needed from her that I couldn't get through email.

Within those few weeks of communication, she said some things that sparked my curiosity and our conversation became more than needing answers; it became a mission to recreate history.

After almost a week of Gloria having my number, she finally decided to call. Her voice sounded as sweet as the day we met in high school and I unexpectedly lost my train of thought. She did something to me no woman had ever been able to do. She had me completely open.

I wanted to be clear about how I felt. I told Gloria I loved her and I had always loved her, even then. We were both bound by marriages, but that didn't stop me from wanting to understand how we got to this point. Gloria asked about my "kids" and that confused me. I'd guessed that since she knew I was married, she assumed I slipped up again and had another baby. But what she said next was the beginning of the end for Sophia and me. She told me that Sophia had reached out to her and told her that she and I had sex around the same timeframe Gloria and I shared our last days together. Sophia also told Gloria that she was expecting another child by me. That whole time I thought she never wanted to speak to me again because Sophia told her she Lewinsky'd me. This news was extremely upsetting and I left work just to confront Sophia.

I kept Gloria on the phone the entire ride home. I needed her to understand all of this was a plot carried out by Sophia and our whole lives could have been different had she not sabotaged our future. When I reached the house, I opted to park in a parking space rather than my garage because it was that urgent that I got in the house as soon as possible. Anyone who knows me knows I wouldn't be caught dead with my car in the general public if I could help it; my cars were my babies.

I busted through the door as Sophia was sitting at the computer stalking Gloria's Facebook images. She looked shocked and asked why I was home so early. The only thing I wanted to know was what she said to Gloria in 2008. As she stood there with a confused face and a bad attitude, Gloria was anxiously trying to get off the phone, repeatedly saying, "You and your wife need to talk. I don't need to be on the phone."

I ignored all of her efforts as I put her on speaker and demanded Sophia to tell her the truth. Sophia refused and reminded me that she was my wife and none of the past should matter.

I wanted to spit in her face and tell her ALL of it mattered. The only thing keeping me from choking her was my Grandma's voice. I could hear her saying, *"A real man would never hurt a woman. There are other ways to show her you're angry. Gentlemen don't make ladies cry."* The only thing was Sophia wasn't a lady in my eyes. She was a fucking monster.

I threw the phone across the room and let out the loudest wail I have ever conjured up. I walked toward the door and before I left, I told Sophia to pack her shit and leave. We were done.

Chapter 13:
Baby, Be Mine

My life took a unexpected turn after I found out it had been tampered with. I found myself wondering what life would have been like if Derric's little senorita wouldn't have made that call that day. I opened my heart back in places that should have only been reserved for Mark. I felt conflicted because although my heart was with Derric, I was still a married woman. We had created a family that I'd always wanted and that Mark had never had. And while I was afraid to lose Derric's love, I was not brave enough to walk away from my family.

Mark and I had made a name for ourselves. We'd starred on two reality shows and people knew us locally and nationally. He was automatically associated with me and vice versa. I felt obligated to our supporters to carry that through, but I felt like I was living a lie. Here I was married to a man that was essentially a fill-in and I was in love with a man that nobody knew about.

My heart was reserved for Derric and my body belonged to Mark. I knew shortly after Mark and I married that he fell short of being able to give me what I needed. I thought I could pray the feeling away or maybe be patient enough for God to turn him into the man that I desired. But the man that I desired was already made; I just wasn't married to him.

Mark and I spent a lot of our marriage figuring things out. We were a blended family and that in itself was a challenge. His baby mommas were bitter and impossible to reason with. For a while it bothered me. I couldn't understand a woman who would interfere with a man's relationship with his child just because she was angry at him for personal issues. I hated the fact that Mark could only see his kids when the mother felt it was necessary. As a woman who grew up without a father, I knew how essential a father/child relationship was and couldn't stand a bitch who would tamper with that.

Aside from having to deal with the baby mommas, as the years went on, Mark and Ka'John began to show signs of disconnect. I would sit back and watch Mark's behavior when dealing with KJ and most of the time, I didn't agree with his tactics. He seemed to get more easily angered at KJ than the other kids; he didn't show as much affection; and he made it a point to always get revenge. I jumped to KJ's defense everytime. After all, he was a surviving child of a father that was deceased. He needed more covering than anyone. Their relationship grew progressively worse.

Mark treated Kase like his own, mostly because he had been around before Kase could talk. I believe their relationship felt more natural than his and Ka'John's. Kase instinctively called Mark, Daddy, and that's what they both felt comfortable with. Chaz was still in hiding when Mark first came around so I didn't have any reason to deny him of that right to be labeled "Dad." It wasn't until our third year into the marriage, when Kase was almost seven, that I was able to track Chaz down.

Chaz had had a change of heart. He found a woman who ultimately changed his life and helped him see the error of his ways. He wanted to right all of his wrongs and claimed to have wanted to start with Kase.

He still wasn't on board to take a paternity test through the county. He was already in the system and knew what they would do to him once they caught up with him. So he opted to start being more present and picking him up on the weekends. Mark and I agreed, but I offered Chaz a private DNA test just so we would have proof for our own records. Really in the back of my mind, I knew he was Chaz's, but confirmation would be comforting. I needed to be able to look my son in the face and tell him the truth confidently.

Chaz eventually agreed to the private test, but dragged it out over the course of a year. I swabbed his mouth and mailed it to the private testing center. I only put only my email on file to get the electronic results because I wanted to be the bearer of the news for him. I knew he didn't want this responsibility and he could have continued to stay in hiding. Mark was doing a fine job raising him as his own and I dreaded the moment of confusion when I had to explain to Kase how Kevin was supposed to be his dad but I fucked up.

A few weeks passed after I submitted the DNA to the testing center when I finally got the email with the results. I opened the email and read it four times before I came to terms with what it said: 0.00000% that Chaz was the father of Kase. I immediately knew this was a mistake. I wasted $125 on a bum ass test for it to give me bogus results. I was in complete denial. Chaz grew curious about the response time and wanted to know if I'd heard anything. I stalled him out until I could come up with a better plan. I eventually told him the results came back inconclusive. He found that suspicious so he took it upon himself to get his own test.

Chaz was excluded from the possibility of being Kase's father after the second test came back with a negative result. I was confused. I became nothing short of those women on Maury screaming, "I'M 1,000% SURE HE DA DADDY."

He couldn't be Kevin's baby; he was brown-skinned and short with slanted eyes and no bridge on his nose. I'd gaze at Kase attentively to see if there were any bits of Kevin in any way. Maybe he got his skin color from my mom's side of the family? I'm short, so maybe he got his height from me. I did everything I could to convince myself I wasn't going crazy.

With all the strain of my marriage and contemplating the what-ifs of Derric, I came to the conclusion I wanted Derric back in my life in some way. He had always been there, regardless of how much I subconsciously or purposefully rejected him. I felt obligated to him. After all, he was there before anyone else in my life.

We began to communicate through text more often. I was more discreet with my notifications and began locking my phone so Mark wouldn't know that Derric and I were talking. I fell right back in that place of comfort with Derric. He fulfilled every emotional need that I wasn't getting from Mark and he seemed to know me better than my own husband. This spoke volumes. Although Derric and I had known each other for years, he still had missed some moments of growth in my life. For him to still know me in that way made me see my life through rose colored glasses.

It didn't help that Mark was lacking in affection and communication. Mark used the excuse that his mom and grandma never hugged him when he was growing up so the lack of endearment stemmed from his childhood. Apparently, that's just how he was raised. I could do the same and argue that I couldn't change how I grew up, but as an adult I chose to take control over my life and change the things I didn't like. I had no tolerance for someone who wanted to be a victim of their circumstance, so much so that it was affecting someone else. After all, he promised before God to give me the things that I needed.

In 2012 Derric's divorce was final. He was serious about what he wanted, and made it clear he wasn't going to make the same mistake again. I felt like I had more to lose; I couldn't just get a divorce. I continued to entertain my marriage while engaging with Derric. I needed something big to happen that would push me over the edge and justify me walking away from my family.

I looked for signs of infidelity with Mark. I knew that he had a wandering eye, and I was sure I'd find something that would even out the score. I monitored all of his social media, text messages and emails, and found nothing. He was disgustingly faithful, which made me look like the crazy, controlling, insecure wife. I held on longer because it was rare for a man to be that faithful, but I couldn't decide which was more important: faithfulness or loyalty. With Mark I had faithfulness, with Derric I had loyalty.

I prayed often. I asked God to show me what I needed to do and who He had for me. I felt conflicted about talking to God about my love triangle since church folks always reminding people that *"God ain't gon' bless no mess."* But God wasn't moving fast enough. Essentially, I took the wheel back. I still very much believed that God would answer my prayers, but I hadn't developed the patience to allow the process to happen the way it was intended.

It had been four years since I had physically touched Derric. My body emotionally shut down to Mark because Derric was completely occupying my heart. He said all the right things, paid attention to my dreams, supported my endeavours and even took steps to help me create realites.

I didn't realize what I was missing until I fully allowed myself to let Derric love me the way that he had always desired. He never gave up on me over all these years. This was the value of unconditional love. I started talking to God about Derric more often and I really only had one request: "If this is Your will, make a way." I prayed that prayer for more than a year before I saw my prayers begin to manifest.

On February 2013, I made a trip to South Carolina to go see Derric. My marriage was falling apart and I began taking heed of the signs I felt like were directly from God.

I had butterflies about seeing Derric again after all this time. Although we kept in touch over the phone and media outlets, my imagination took me to a place that could only be fulfilled by his familiar touch. When I arrived at his place, I was greeted with a sign on the door that simply said: Come in.

I walked in to find a trail of 11 yellow roses and one red rose at the end that led to a folded note with my name on it. Mary J. Blige and Method man were playing in the background and I began to open the note to Mary blaring, *"You're alllll I need, to get byyyy."*

The note was an apology letter for skipping steps to capture my heart. He wanted me to excuse him from the moments he missed out on because of his lack of knowledge and fear of confrontation with me. The note went on to say he always loved me from the moment he met me and he didn't want to have any more space between us. The note was amusingly signed by his mother.

As I looked up, I saw my reflection in a mirror. I caught a glimpse of myself smiling so joyfully, I could see all the teeth in my mouth at the same time. Derric stuck his head to the side of the mirror and exclaimed this was how he wanted to make me smile for the rest of my life. He said he wanted the opportunity to love me, uninterrupted. I melted in his arms and felt a weight lift off me. I didn't realize I was waiting all of this time to exhale.

I pulled back and looked Derric in his eyes for more than a few minutes. It was like I could see right to his heart, his authenticity seeping through his pores. I studied his slanted eyes, his brown skin, his bridgeless nose, and the mole above his right eye. I didn't realize how aesthetically pleasing his face was until then. It's amazing how I was blinded all those years by personal idea of what I thought love should look like, act like, talk like.

We sat for hours reminiscing and talking about the what-ifs. We settled things that were pressing and compared our hindsight. We talked about all the missed opportunities and confessed things that neither one of us wanted to hear, but were important puzzle pieces.

Derric admitted he came into town in late 2006 with the intention of checking on me after Kevin's passing, and backed out because he was overwhelmed with my unexpected pregnancy. He then proceeded to go down a path I was trying to avoid. I wasn't ready to talk to him about Kase. I was ashamed that I didn't have answers and that Kase was not Kevin's son. I didn't want to have to tell him about Chaz or any other rendezvous.

He expressed his frustrations about that whole situation exclaiming he didn't understand how in that same year on Valentine's day, we could share a moment of intimacy and I turn around and get pregnant by another man. My heart dropped. Not just because of his aggressive assertion, but because I completely forgot about us making love that night.

As Derric was talking, I was rapidly counting back in my head months from the time Kase was born to when Derric and I had sex, then back from the time we had sex, back to the time Kase was born. My mind couldn't rest. Two hundred eighty days in a pregnancy, 40 weeks, 10 months, four trimesters, one penis. I took a step back and looked at Derric. I was sick. For almost 8 years, I had carried a piece of him with me and didn't even realize it. Kase was undeniably Derric's child.

I stood there shook. All the blood rushed away from my face and my eyes were focused on recounting all of the birthdays and holidays that had been missed. This would be the straw that broke the camel's back. I'd already denied him of his right to his unborn child. Now I had unknowingly detained a child that was alive and well with whom he could have loved on for the past seven years.

I didn't move. I only began to cry out to God and question His motives. Derric stood close by, confused and seemingly nervous at my outburst. I finally dropped to my knees as if to release all the power I had been holding onto for all my life. I kneeled powerless and as I cried frantically, I asked God to take me on home as I would rather die before I hurt Derric again.

He said

Chapter 13:
Baby, Be Mine

I thought I would suffer through my marriage with Sophia until Pedro turned 18. I was reluctantly willing to try because I knew the type of person Sophia was and I knew that she would not only make the relationship with my son harder to maintain, but she would also try and suck me dry financially. After I found out what she did, I didn't feel as though she deserved anything; not even a comfortable place to stay. She was never the type of woman that added to my life. She only found ways to take from me. My money, my son, my pride, and now, Gloria.

After finding out about Sophia's maliciousness, I knew that it was no longer possible to continue living the way that I had been living. When I told Gloria that I was going to divorce Sophia, I thought we were on the same page and that she would immediately divorce Mark. But instead, she decided to stick around because she claimed in the past she'd made selfish decisions and now she was trying to listen to God and do the right thing.

I knew for sure God hated me. I was never the "right thing" for her. I felt like I suffered for all these years to wait for a woman who didn't love me as much as I loved her. I couldn't understand how she could tell me that she loved me and wanted to be with me, then turn around and tell me she wanted to stay in a false marriage. I felt like history was repeating itself.

I didn't feel the same way towards Mark as I did towards Kevin. With Kevin I felt like I just didn't measure up to him, creating a huge complex. I wanted to know why wasn't I good enough for Gloria. Although it was hurtful to play second fiddle to Kevin while he was alive, it was damaging to get passed over for Mark. Neither one of these niggas loved her or reverenced her the way I did.

Gloria was with Mark by default, thanks to Sophia. Seeing Gloria all over TV with this happenstance ass nigga made me HATE Sophia. I couldn't help but feel tremendous hostility toward her that wouldn't go away.

There were many days I was physically ill and considered smashing all of my TVs. I canceled all of my social media accounts just so there wouldn't be a living chance I would have to see Gloria and Mark's images.

Granted, I'd married Sophia, but she metaphorically held a gun to my head. I'd thought Gloria would never speak to me again, so I settled for a carbon copy of Brandi Web from *It's A Thin line Between Love and Hate.* Being in a situation with someone that I didn't like as a person, let alone a wife, and knowing that I was only there because I had no choice but to settle, made my days seem dark. To add insult to injury, finding out that the only person on earth I have ever loved so deeply was married to some random ass nobody.

Mark got ahold of my number a few times. He was apparently going through Gloria's phone and came across some of our text messages. My first thoughts of Mark once I had actually talked to him was that he had a lot of feminine traits. What grown man goes through a woman's phone with intentions on gathering evidence and building a case? I could tell he had been monitoring her phone for a while because he mentioned some dated things. Real men are just built different, we run up on shit.

Mark threatened to kill me if I ever reached out to "his wife" again. All I could do was shrug it off. Technically she *was* his wife. Even though I didn't really care for Mark, I did realize that none of it was actually his fault. Mark was a victim of circumstance, collateral damage. Gloria chose him out of perceived necessity. He was her "safe choice." Mark was the rebound guy that made it to marriage and kids, but he was never right for her.

Although Gloria said she was going to work out her marriage, she still found ways to string me along. Somehow I became her relationship therapist, confidante, and best friend. I never gave her advice on how to keep her marriage together, I only listened as she confessed it was falling apart. Gloria mentioned many times that she didn't want to leave Mark for me, she wanted to put forth all her efforts toward making her marriage work out. And if at that point she and Mark didn't work out, *then* we could try again.

Meanwhile, I was going through a beastly divorce off the strength of a lie that had compromised my relationship with Gloria.

But who was I kidding? I would have eventually divorced Sophia for much less. My relationship with Pedro started to suffer. He was at a critical age where he was susceptible to everything and I was pretty sure that Sophia was putting bullshit in his head. As a father, I became unsure of myself and the decisions I was making. Sophia almost convinced me that I was fucking up my life and certainly Pedro's life. As hard as it was to deny my son of the only family unit he had ever known, I found the strength to walk away.

Mentally Sophia wanted me to believe I was fucked up. Spiritually she wanted me to believe I was going to burn in hell. And verbally, she never held her tongue. I couldn't wait to quote James 3:11 to her face: "Can both freshwater and salt water flow from the same spring? Huh, bitch!?" I wanted to show her what the definition of a sanctimonious person was. She always wanted to hit me in the head with the Bible, but wasn't living her best life.

On top of all of the maltreatment from Sophia, Gloria was quickly killing me emotionally.

I left my condo and rented an apartment three miles from the house Sophia and I shared. Despite all the deadbeats and broken loser labels I inherited from her, ironically she was still living in a home I owned and that I continued to pay the mortgage for. But she insisted I owed her at least that much since I filed for the divorce. At that time, I was desperate to rid myself of her, so I was always as brief and docile as possible. It took almost two years to finalize our divorce, but by the end of 2012, I was a free man.

I missed Gloria incredibly. Although I didn't have Sophia nagging in my ear constantly by this time, I still ended up losing more than I bargained for. I only got to see Pedro twice a month and none of my phone calls would ever get through when I wanted to talk to him. I cut all my friends off and I barely talked to my family. All I did was go to work, watch TV and sleep.

Work was starting to get more challenging because I had a lot of down time to think. During idle time, I start thinking about my failures. My depression got worse and I felt the weight of the world on me. I cried more that year than any other time in my life. I was an emotional wreck.

As a man, it was hard to come to terms with these feelings, but hitting the bottom left no room for pride. It was extremely hard for me to function in everyday life. There were plenty of days where I thought I wasn't going to make it.

In early 2013, I had a dream that would ultimately change my life. In the dream, I saw my father and I felt all the hurt and pain of my childhood rush back at me. I was so angry with this man for abandoning me that I began to strike him. Surprisingly he fought back and we began to scuffle. It seemed like we fought all night and I was getting the best of him until he hit me with a cheap shot in my ribs.

My body was weak, but I refused to let go until something changed. I felt like he was responsible for how my life turned out, all the poor choices I'd made, the lack of wisdom I'd possessed, and all the insecurities. I held on until I heard a child calling for their daddy. The small voice scared me and it came from all directions. Finally, a little girl appeared.

She had red hair and freckles, and appeared to be about nine years old. I stepped away from my father to get a better look at this little girl who called *me* Daddy. I asked her why and she simply said, "Because that's who you are to me."

The little girl walked away, smiling and whispering, "You are free. You are free." I turned around and my father was standing there with a boy child who looked much like me when I was a young. My dad was kneeling down speaking to him face to face. He was apologizing to the child for his unguarded and forsaking ways. He called the child Dionte and held him close until they both disappeared.

I woke up with a heavy heart, but with a peace that surpassed all understanding. As I tried to piece the dream together, my grandma happened to call and the ringer from my cell phone almost caused me to piss my pants. I quickly answered, trying to straighten out my shaky voice so she wouldn't pick up on any vexation. The first thing she said was, "Hey Dionte baby, I was thinking about you. Do you have enough clean underwear for the week?" My grandma always called me by my middle name.

I couldn't help but believe that God was sending me a message through this dream. I had held onto anger for my father that had been eating me alive. I had tried my hardest to become everything he was not, and avoid everything he was, but in the midst of fighting myself, I seemed to also be fighting God.

My grandma used to always tell me that unforgiveness is like drinking poison and expecting the other person to die. Those words didn't become real until I realized he wasn't going to die just because I despised him. I never wanted my father to "die," but I certainly wanted him to hurt enough to feel my pain.

I thought about the baby Gloria aborted. I knew that was my baby girl in that dream. She was beautiful. I wanted to hold her and tell her I was sorry for never getting the opportunity to love her. I wanted to tell her I've always thought about her, what she would have looked like, and if she would have taken on some of her mother's characteristics. I had always known she was a girl. She had a glow about her that was angelic. She wasn't upset; she wasn't hurt. She seemed happy.

Things were notably different after the night of my dream. I felt weights lifting off me as I released anger and resentment. It's almost as if God decided to take His foot off my neck. Things seemed to be shifting. Life seemed to make more sense once I started to let go of the things that were keeping me in bondage. As my grandma was always saying, "Love covers a multitude of sins" and "Forgiveness is for *you*, not the other person."

As a child, I couldn't appreciate the parable lessons my grandma fed to me. And I hadn't realized how well they stuck with me throughout my life until then. I didn't understand that the lessons being instilled in me would one day be shields for the weapons that tried to form against me.

I decided to call my father. Before that moment, I hadn't desired to speak to him. I was angry and felt like he owed me something.

That same year, Gloria came to Charleston to see me. I decided it was now or never. I'd waited 14 years for her to choose me and I was determined to end the cycle of cat and mouse. We didn't come this far just to come this far. She had finally determined her marriage was over and felt God was clear with His intentions to bring us together. I had my mind made up that there was nothing or no one that would come between us this time. No matter what Gloria said to intentionally or unintentionally to sabotage our future, at the end of the day, I was going to do what I should have done many years ago and ask her to be my wife.

God said

Chapter 14:
Final Say

Gloria:

My child, before I formed you in the womb, I knew you. Before you were born, I set you apart; I appointed you as a prophet to the nations. A father to the fatherless, a defender of widows, am I in my holy dwellings. I will be a father to you, and you will be my daughter. I have said these things to you, that in me, you may have peace. In the world you will have tribulation, but take heart; I have overcome the world for I consider that the sufferings of this present time are not worth comparing with the glory that is to be revealed to you.

You will call upon me and come and pray to me, and I will hear you. You will seek me and find me, when you seek me with your whole heart. I sent you someone who saw you, an imperfect person, perfectly. Who loved you in spite of you, who forgave you, who loved you unconditionally, who never left you or forsook you, and who would ultimately be willing to die for you... sound familiar?

Count it all joy when you meet trials of various kinds, for you know that the testing of your faith produces steadfastness. And let steadfastness have its full effect, that you may be perfect and complete, lacking nothing. Three times you pleaded with me, and I replied to you, "My grace is sufficient for you, for my power is made perfect in weakness, so my power may rest upon you."

Be content with weaknesses, insults, hardships, persecutions and calamities. For when you are weak, then you are strong. Rejoice in this. Though now you have been grieved by various trials, so that the tested genuineness of your faith, more precious than gold that perishes though it is tested by fire, may be found to result in praise and glory and honor at the revelation of Christ.

No temptation has overtaken you that is not common to man. I am faithful and will not let you be tempted beyond your ability, but with temptation I will also provide the way of escape, that you may be able to endure it. After you have suffered a little while, I will restore, confirm, strengthen, and establish you.

Derric:

My son, I have not forgotten about you, but even the hairs of your hair are all numbered. Don't be afraid. You are more valuable than many sparrows. Cast all your anxieties on me because I care for you. Your father may have forsaken you, but I will take you in. Get wisdom; get insight; do not forget and do not turn away from the words of my mouth. I know the plans I have for you. I declare, plans of welfare and not for evil, to give you future and hope.

Son, do not believe every spirit, but test the spirits to see whether they are from me. Many false prophets have gone out into the world. Let all you do be done in love. Humble yourself, therefore, under my mighty hand, that I may lift you up in due time.

Beware of the beautiful woman who lacks discretion. She is like a gold ring in a pig's snout. She has a seductive, persuasive and evil mouth. The lips of an immoral woman are as sweet as honey and her mouth is smoother than oil. But in the end, she is bitter as poison, as dangerous as a double-edged sword. It is better to live in a corner of a housetop than in a house shared with a quarrelsome wife.

I created you to be more like Jacob, serving seven years for Rachel. Your real bride will not be ready. She is still Leah. You must serve another seven years as I prepare her to become your Rachel. Do not forsake her and she will guard you. The beginning of wisdom is this: get wisdom, and whatever you get, get insight. Prize her highly and she will exalt you. She will honor you if you embrace her. She will place on your head a graceful garland; she will bestow on you a beautiful crown. And we know that for those who love God, all things work together for good, for those who are called according to His purpose.

God is love. Whoever lives in love lives in God and God in them. There is no fear in love, but perfect love drives out fear because fear has to do with punishment. The one who fears is not made perfect in love. Love is patient; love is kind; love does not envy or boast; it is not arrogant or rude. It does not insist on its own way; it is not irritable or resentful; it does not rejoice at wrongdoing, but rejoices with the truth. Love bears all things, believes all things, hopes all things, endures all things. Love never ends.

Made in the USA
Columbia, SC
28 October 2020